The Climax of Populism

ROBERT F. DURDEN

The
Climax of Populism:
The Election of
1896

KENTUCKY PAPERBACKS
UNIVERSITY OF KENTUCKY PRESS
Lexington, 1966

To my mother
MILDRED DONALDSON DURDEN
and to
my late father
VIRGIL EDWARD DURDEN
who shared and stimulated
my first interest in
the Populists

Preface

SELDOM in American history has a third political party had such impact on contemporary events and been the object of such continuing interest among historians as the People's party, or Populists, of the 1890's. The colorful characteristics of some of the leaders of the party—largely an agrarian one —are by no means the sole reason for the continuing attention the party receives. Although the flamboyance and eccentricity of a few "Pops" caused conservatives at the time, and some historians since, to ridicule them as provincial cranks, by no means all of the Populist leaders were "sockless," as an enemy dubbed Congressman Jerry Simpson of Kansas.

A young Populist leader and United States Senator from North Carolina, Marion Butler, played a central role in the political events of 1896. Although he certainly had a farm background, as did well over half of the American people at the time, Butler was graduated from the University of North Carolina. And he was, like many of his coworkers in the People's party, an educated man of considerable dignity and polish.

Not their alleged eccentricities then, but the reform ideas and efforts of the Populists account for their lasting importance. Their demands foreshadowed a considerable part of the achievements of the Progressives and New Dealers in the twentieth century. In their own time, the Populists exerted great influence not only in the southern and western states where they were strongest but also on the political life of the nation as a whole.

They played a leading role in the rise to ascendancy of the free silver issue and, obliquely, in the revolution within the Democratic party epitomized by the nomination of William Jennings Bryan in 1896. In the campaign that followed, easily the most significant one that the nation had known since 1865, the Populists occupied strategic ground and, mainly, made their greatest national effort for Bryan, whom they also nominated as their presidential candidate, and for the various reforms that free silver symbolized.

Despite many studies of different aspects of the "Battle of the Standards" in 1896, confusion and error persist concerning the role of the People's party. According to many historical accounts, the Populists were tricked by wily leaders into nominating Bryan and allegedly expressed their deepest and truest desires only in the nomination of Thomas E. Watson of Georgia as their own vice-presidential candidate. In the accounts of the campaign itself, most historians depict Watson as the ill-treated martyr of Populism who was betrayed not only by false Democratic promises but more especially by devious Populist leaders.

A quite different perspective on the Populist part in the epochal campaign of 1896 is furnished by the study of a large collection of documents in the Southern Historical Collection of the University of North Carolina Library. These are the papers of Marion Butler, who played a decisive role in the controversial Populist convention in St. Louis and was elected at the conclusion of that meeting as the national chairman of the People's party. Hundreds of letters that came to Chairman Butler from Populists all over the nation during the campaign, together with two thick letterbooks of his outgoing correspondence, afford an inside view and a new understanding of the Populist effort both in the nation and in most of the states where the third party flourished.

The two most important studies dealing with the Populists

in 1896 remain Professor John Hicks' *The Populist Revolt,*
which was first published in 1931, and Professor C. Vann
Woodward's *Tom Watson: Agrarian Rebel,* which appeared
in 1938. Professor Hicks' book continues to be the most
comprehensive account of the subject, as is evidenced by the
fact that it was reprinted in 1961, and is still widely used in
libraries and classrooms, including my own. Professor Woodward's biography of Watson has also been recently reissued
and has come to be recognized as a classic portrayal of a social
class and a section almost as much as a study of its fascinating
subject. *Tom Watson,* it so happens, was the first book in
American history about which I remember becoming deeply
and personally excited. The Butler papers were not available,
however, when these two distinguished historians published
their Populist studies, and both portray the Populist convention and the ensuing campaign in a manner quite different
from that which follows.

The purpose of this book, then, is to show first that the
Populists were not tricked into naming Bryan as their candidate and that there was no "conspiracy" at the St. Louis
convention. Rather, the Populists' nomination of the Nebraskan Democrat was not only consistent with their principles but was essential if the party was to remain national in
scope. In the campaign itself, despite embarrassment caused
by Tom Watson, who had allowed himself to be sadly miscast
in the political drama, the national leaders of the Populists
worked out a largely effective policy of electoral-ticket fusion
with the Democrats. And this policy made possible both the
preservation of the Populist national and state organizations
and the participation by the Populists in the great allied effort
for Bryan and national reforms. The year 1896, in short, saw
the climax of Populism, the time of its greatest significance
in American history.

That McKinley and the status quo triumphed over Bryan

and reform was not because of any failure of the Populists. They, together with their political allies for silver, concentrated their efforts in the campaign on the farmers and industrial workers in the pivotal north central states. And there, through circumstances largely beyond the control of the reform parties, the reformers lost their first great bid for progressive change.

Mostly farmers, the Populists were not spokesmen for a static society, nor were they opposing and fleeing from the industrial future of the nation. They sought rather to capture federal power and use it both negatively to end economic abuses that had flourished since the Civil War and positively to improve the lot of the farmers and industrial workers of the land. The Populists failed in 1896—but their failure was by no means ignominious, and in one sense they triumphed at a later day when their reforms were introduced under other auspices and the "Pops" had become but a fading memory.

Perhaps two other points should be made here about the intensely human and political story that follows. First, political "spoils" in the form of salaried offices, high and low, did play a large part in the politics of the 1890's, larger perhaps than is true of our own prosperous day. This fact was true of the Populists just as it was of the Democrats and Republicans, and it did not mean that Americans were then more venal or selfish. The reason was simple: the depression that began in 1893 was merely the lowest point in a deflationary cycle that reached far back into the Gilded Age. Incredibly low farm prices, unemployment, and grinding poverty made many men desperate for an office—almost any office— that paid a fixed salary in an era when the dollar grew scarcer as its purchasing power increased.

Secondly, the truism that ours is a federal system of politics as well as of government needs repeating in advance. The Populists' struggles to reconcile their conflicting sectional interests with their national organization and policies led to an amazing complexity in the election of 1896. Indeed, the infinite variety of politics in the United States has never been more strikingly demonstrated. The reader who remembers that American political parties are not and have never been primarily concerned about their ideological purity and that they are composed of many state and sectional units rather than being national monoliths will appreciate rather than deplore some of the aspects of the climactic struggle of the Populists.

Fortunately, the Research Council of Duke University has patience in good supply. The Council began to assist my summertime research into Populism some ten years ago. When other projects developed and caused long interruptions, the Council raised no objections. It is a pleasure to thank them and particularly the chairman, Professor John Tate Lanning.

The most important documents for this study were in the Southern Historical Collection of the University of North Carolina Library, and Dr. James W. Patton, the director of the Collection, and Dr. Carolyn Wallace of his staff were particularly helpful. Dr. Mattie Russell, director of the Manuscript Division of the Duke University Library, gave assistance ungrudgingly and others in the Duke Library who helped were Miss Florence Blakely, Miss Mary Canada, Mr. Emerson Ford, Mr. Elvin Strowd, and Mr. Peter Tavernise. Likewise the staffs of the Newspaper and Manuscript Divisions of the Library of Congress, the Wisconsin State Historical Society, the Minnesota State Historical Society, and the State Library of North Carolina facilitated my work.

In Duke University, Professors Hugh M. Hall, William B. Hamilton, I. B. Holley, William T. Laprade, Richard H. Leach, Anne F. Scott, and Richard L. Watson have kindly read all or parts of the manuscript, which Mrs. Elizabeth

McConnell helped to type. A number of students over the years have shared ideas about the Populists and 1896, but Mr. David Roller and Mr. Bruce Clayton were of special assistance in certain aspects of the research. My wife, Anne Oller Durden, transcribed documents with me in Wisconsin and Minnesota and shared the chore of indexing.

Portions of the first two chapters of this book have appeared in substantially different form in the *Mississippi Valley Historical Review* and the *South Atlantic Quarterly*.

Duke University   ROBERT F. DURDEN
August 1963

Contents

1

The Crisis for Populism

ALTHOUGH some historians disparage both William Jennings Bryan and the demand for free silver, few deny the significance of the election of 1896. The cry for reform, raised sporadically since the late 1860's, had grown into a massive roar. Instead of continuing the duet about the tariff that economic conservatives had sung meaninglessly at every election for a generation, the new elements which had captured the Democratic party clamorously advocated change. Frightened friends of the status quo rallied behind the comfortable conservatism of William McKinley and his astute manager, Marcus A. Hanna. The mere possibility of the changes threatened by the Bryan Democracy drove a large faction of Cleveland Democrats out of the party and into either direct or indirect support of McKinley. The overwhelming majority of the American people at the time, on both sides of the politico-economic fence, believed deeply that the issues involved were fundamental ones.

The story of the first Bryan-McKinley campaign is complicated, however, by the fact that the People's party played a significant role in it. The Populists were important in the rise to ascendancy of the silver question; they were a factor even in the Democrats' selection of Bryan; and they figured largely in the campaign and election that brought his first defeat for the presidency. Although much has been written about the clash of the "silverites" and the "goldbugs," misunderstanding and plain error have persisted concerning the role of the Populists.[1]

Basic to any understanding of 1896 is the currency question. Some weeks after the Populist convention Henry Demarest Lloyd, a leading reformer and famed author, called free silver "the cow-bird of the Reform movement." "It waited until the nest had been built by the sacrifices and labour of others," Lloyd charged, "and then it laid its eggs in it, pushing out the others which lie smashed on the ground."[2]

Influential historians have quoted and endorsed Lloyd's interpretation, but his denunciation of the silver issue is misleading in several ways.[3] Lloyd was a socialist, committed to government ownership of the means of production and distribution as the great principle that would bring justice to all. He joined the People's party in an effort to unite under its banner both industrial workers and agrarians and

[1] A critical discussion of the most important printed works that deal with the Populists in the election of 1896 is given in the Note on Sources. Two full-length studies that are available to scholars should be mentioned here: Marian Silveus, "The Antecedents of the Campaign of 1896," unpublished dissertation at the University of Wisconsin (1932), is useful in many respects but collapses in its treatment of the Populist convention. Relying only on the New York *Times* for the story, Silveus admits (p. 225) that it was "impossible to tell just what did happen." Joseph Schafer, Jr., "The Presidential Election of 1896," unpublished dissertation at the University of Wisconsin (1941), also has merit but, with respect to the Populist convention and its action, closely follows the interpretation of two important leaders, Henry D. Lloyd and Tom Watson. For reasons that are explained below, both of these men had highly distorted views of the matter.

[2] Lloyd to A. B. Adair, October 10, 1896, in the Lloyd MSS, State Historical Society of Wisconsin.

[3] Selected examples of historians who incorporate Lloyd's "cow-bird" thesis are, in order of publication: C. Vann Woodward, *Tom Watson: Agrarian Rebel* (New York, 1938), 278; Matthew Josephson, *The Politicos, 1865-1896* (New York, 1938), 684; Richard Hofstadter, *The American Political Tradition and the Men Who Made It* (New York, 1948), 189; Eric F. Goldman, *Rendezvous with Destiny: A History of Modern American Reform* (New York, 1953), 56; Harold U. Faulkner, *Politics, Reform and Expansion, 1890-1900* in the New American Nation series (New York, 1959), 199; and Paul W. Glad, *McKinley, Bryan, and the People* (Philadelphia, 1964), 163 and *passim*.

to lead the Populists to a gradual acceptance of socialism.[4]

Although the Populists had incorporated a demand for government ownership of the railroads and telegraphs in their Omaha platform of 1892, neither they nor the Farmers' Alliance men were doctrinaire socialists. They were, rather, angry agrarian capitalists who found themselves unprotected by government from exploitation by the railroads. They responded with a pragmatic demand for government ownership, a demand that made many of them uncomfortable but which persisted until federal regulation became a meaningful reality in the twentieth century.

Lloyd, on the other hand, advocated government ownership to establish a different economic and social order. Even in comparatively urban Illinois, Lloyd's efforts came to naught many months before the Populist convention in 1896.[5] Herman E. Taubeneck, chairman of the Populist national committee, spoke both for the agrarians and for some of the urban workers when he greeted Lloyd's collectivist proposal with the declaration that if "this is what you came into the People's party for, we don't want you. Go back where you came [from] with your socialism."[6]

[4] Caro Lloyd, *Henry Demarest Lloyd, 1847-1903* (2 vols.; New York, 1912), I, 241-43.

[5] At a Populist-sponsored conference in Springfield in May 1894, advocates of "Plank 10," calling for government ownership of the means of production and distribution, made a determined effort to have the idea endorsed. Representatives from the Illinois State Federation of Labor, the Socialist Labor Party, the Knights of Labor, and other urban-industrial organizations attended along with the Populist delegates. Plank 10 was overwhelmingly rejected. Chester M. Destler, *American Radicalism, 1865-1901* (New London, Conn., 1946), 170. This earlier work of Professor Destler's is more useful and sounder on Lloyd's role as a Populist than the same author's recent biography, *Henry Demarest Lloyd and the Empire of Reform* (Philadelphia, 1963).

[6] Illinois *State Register*, May 30, 1894, quoted in Destler, *American Radicalism*, 170. In July 1894 the Illinois State Federation of Labor at first rejected Plank 10 but for the sake of harmony "a sugar coated edition of 'Plank 10' was adopted chiefly through the instrumentality of Henry D. Lloyd." This called for collective ownership of all such means of production and distribution "as the people elect to operate for the commonwealth."

Even one of Lloyd's friends and coworkers, the young
Clarence Darrow, questioned socialist tactics in trying to
capture the People's party. Lloyd insisted that the "People's
Party platform is socialistic as all democratic doctrine is."
But Darrow had misgivings "as to whether we could claim
to commit the People[']s party to Socialism." "I think it was
done too much in the last campaign," Darrow continued;
"for instance all the literature circulated at the meeting was
intensely socialistic such as the 'People's party' would not
indorse and as it was under their auspices it ought not to
have been such as was antagonistic to a large portion of the
party."[7]

Though Lloyd persisted, the national convention of the
American Federation of Labor, meeting in Denver late in
1894, rejected his collectivist proposals. Lloyd did better at a
conference of Populist leaders at St. Louis in December
1894, when he was one of the spokesmen who helped lead
the majority to stand by the comprehensive and many-sided
Populist platform of 1892 rather than retreat to the silver-
only position that some of the western Populists favored.
But despite the fluctuations in his hopes, Lloyd's plan to
unite workers and farmers in a party dedicated to socialism
failed even in the area and under the circumstances most
auspicious for the effort. In 1895, Henry Vincent, a Populist
editor in Indiana who had earlier sympathized with a part of
Lloyd's program, warned that the "Socialists in their arrogant
assumption are looking upon the People's party with much
the same contemplation that a boa constrictor looks upon
the beast he is shadowing for an early morning meal." If a
Populist such as Vincent rejected socialism, even when it was

Edward B. Mittleman, "Chicago Labor in Politics, 1877-1896," *Journal of
Political Economy*, XXVIII (May 1920), 424-25.
[7] Lloyd to Darrow, November 23, 1894, and Darrow to Lloyd, "Saturd[a]y,"
quoted in Destler, *American Radicalism*, 232.

diluted and brilliantly presented by a humane intellectual such as Lloyd, small wonder that the overwhelming majority of the agrarian Populists in the West and South would have no part of it.[8]

Tom Watson of Georgia, perhaps the best known figure among the Populists of the South, spoke for the bulk of his party late in 1895 when he vowed that he would go no further toward "Socialism and Radicalism" than the Georgia Populists had gone. That group, Watson reported to Marion Butler, had given the "cold shoulder" even to the doctrines of Jacob S. ("Good Roads") Coxey of Ohio and had adopted the "most conservative" platform that the party had ever had. Watson urged that Butler and others who favored a moderate course should begin to use their newspapers to educate public sentiment and thus make it impossible for extremists to control the forthcoming national convention. That important gathering would need a chairman who "has nerve enough to rule with a rod of iron those hot-headed recalcitrants who want to load us down with extreme isms." Prophetically, and ironically in view of subsequent developments, Watson at that stage thought that William V. Allen, Populist senator from Nebraska, or Marion Butler himself would be good men to wield the "rod of iron" against the extremists.[9]

Too much should not be made of Watson's comments to Butler. Serious differences existed about ideology and strategy even among the antisocialist Populists. The point remains, however, that to most Populists the real, late-coming "cow-

[8] *Ibid.*, 230-34, 243. Lloyd was apparently either ignorant of southern Populism or unsympathetic with it. He wrote to A. B. McCulloch of Richmond, Virginia, on January 9, 1896, that: "I had supposed until I became acquainted with all this [activity in Richmond] that there was absolutely no radical thought in the South. But lately the evidences have multiplied that it is farther advanced than I had believed." Lloyd MSS.

[9] Watson to Butler, December 23, 28, 1895, in the Marion Butler MSS, Southern Historical Collection, University of North Carolina Library.

bird" of 1896 that tried to capture the Populist nest was socialism. As Professor Chester Destler has concluded, the fate of the "attempt to graft an alien collectivism into the traditional pattern of American democratic radicalism had been clearly foreshadowed in Chicago."[10] Lloyd would not know how completely that attempt had failed until the Populist convention in July 1896. His widely quoted and influential comments about the action of that body reflect his own final, bitter disillusionment more accurately than they do the truth about the Populist convention and the free silver movement.

The history of the silver issue cannot be dealt with here, but a few general points must be made.[11] The demand for the free coinage of silver was not a late addition to the reform movement of the 1890's. A free silver plank was always among the numerous demands first of the Farmers' Alliance and then of the People's party. Agitation of the question reached back to the 1870's; and from 1868 on there was opposition to the federal government's deflationary moves that led to the steady appreciation of the dollar's value. Events rather than planning by any person or group forced the silver issue irresistibly to the front in the mid-1890's.

Two of these events were the catastrophic depression that followed the panic of 1893 and the stubbornly conservative, deflationary, probusiness, and party-splitting policies of the Democratic administration of Grover Cleveland. Neither the Populists nor the Bryan Democrats created the popular clamor for the restoration of silver to its historic place in the currency. Rather, the leaders of both groups were led by popular sentiment to emphasize the issue.

[10] Destler, *American Radicalism*, 254.
[11] Lucid accounts may be found in Elmer Ellis, *Henry Moore Teller: Defender of the West* (Caldwell, Idaho, 1941), 184 ff., and Paolo E. Coletta, "Greenbackers, Goldbugs, and Silverites: Currency, Reform and Policy, 1860-1897," in H. Wayne Morgan (ed.), *The Gilded Age: A Reappraisal* (Syracuse, 1963), 111-39.

Long before the silverites captured the Democratic party in 1896, the Populists had discovered in the campaign of 1892 that among their numerous demands the silver plank had the greatest popular appeal.[12] True, a majority of the Populists were not willing to eliminate demands for other important reforms. But Populist leaders were no different from those of the older parties in yielding to the drift of voters' opinions. B. O. Flower, editor of *The Arena*, one of the few national magazines that supported Populism and reform in general, advised Marion Butler late in 1894 that wise action by the Populists would bring them victory in 1896. Flower wanted the Populists to continue to educate the people on all lines of reform but especially to emphasize the money question now that Cleveland had brought to a climax the life-and-death struggle between the "money power" and the people. "No more class legislation, more money and less misery," would be the winning slogan according to Flower.[13]

Marion Butler needed no urging. As the acknowledged leader of the Populists in North Carolina and president of the National Farmers' Alliance and Industrial Union, he had clearly demonstrated the capacity for adroit political leadership. Born on a farm in Sampson County in southeastern North Carolina in 1863, Butler was one of a significant number of young men who rose rapidly in the political flux created by the agrarian revolt of the 1890's. Despite the poverty that afflicted Tarheel farmers in the years after the Civil War, he managed to graduate from the University of North Carolina in 1885. His plans to study law at the University were cut short, however, when his father died, and Butler, still in his early twenties, had to assume the responsibility for running the family farm.

---

[12] John D. Hicks, *The Populist Revolt: A History of the Farmers' Alliance and the People's Party* (Lincoln, Nebr., 1961), 301.
[13] Flower to Butler, December 14, 1894, Butler MSS.

In addition to farming, Butler conducted an academy for
the schooling of his younger brothers and sisters together
with the children of neighbors. When the Farmers' Alliance
movement, destined to become the most militant agrarian
combination in American history, spread from the Southwest
into North Carolina in the late 1880's, Marion Butler immediately joined the organization, which provided him a
ladder of political opportunity that he climbed with amazing
speed. Possessing the formal education and literate articulate-
ness which so many of his fellow farmers lacked, he quickly
became president of the Sampson County Alliance, bought a
weekly newspaper in the county seat of Clinton (the newspaper was subsequently moved to Goldsboro and then to
Raleigh), and in 1890, at the age of twenty-seven, the voters
sent him to the state senate as an Alliance Democrat.[14]

The "Farmers' Legislature" of 1891 in North Carolina
produced an impressive number of important reform measures,
such as the creation of a commission to regulate the railroads
and the establishment of new state colleges for women and
Negroes. Through his dynamic leadership in the legislature,
Butler established a statewide reputation. He became president of the State Farmers' Alliance in 1891, and was made,
first, vice president and then, in 1893, president of the National Alliance. The Democratic nomination of Grover Cleveland in 1892, despite the former president's known hostility
to silver and his essential conservatism, was a major factor
behind the organization of the People's party in North
Carolina in the summer of 1892. Another factor was the
insistence of the leaders of the North Carolina Democratic
party that no member could "split the ticket," that is, vote
Democratic in the state and local elections but not in the
presidential race. Thousands of members of the Alliance,

---

[14] Samuel A. Ashe and others, eds., *Biographical History of North Carolina*
(Greensboro, N. C., 1917), VIII, 81-90.

now led by young Butler after the death of Colonel Leonidas L. Polk in June 1892, took a step that required considerable courage and even desperation in the South after Reconstruction: they walked out of the "white man's party," the party that had "redeemed" the South from Republican rule in the Reconstruction era, and they joined the new third party that had already developed in the West and was now appearing in both the upper and deep South.[15]

The Populist presidential candidate in 1892, General James B. Weaver of Iowa, polled over a million popular votes and won twenty-two electoral votes, which was an impressive showing for a new third party. In North Carolina the Populists entered the campaign too late to hope for much, yet the Tarheel Populists and Republicans together polled a larger vote than the Democrats, whose penny-pinching economies and exclusive claims to "honesty and good government" during the two decades since Reconstruction had clearly lost much of their appeal. Marion Butler now emerged as the nemesis of North Carolina Democrats, who tagged him "the sly fox of Sampson county," for in the state elections of 1894 he led the Populists into cooperation with the Republicans.

Both Populists and Republicans deeply resented the tricky, even dishonest, election laws and procedures that the Democrats had utilized to remain in power since Reconstruction; both also scorned the centralization of all political power in the legislature whereby Democrats monopolized local offices in numerous counties where their opponents had strong majorities. In order to gain reforms in these and other state matters, and simply for the satisfaction of beating the Democrats, the Populist-Republican "fusionists," as their enemies called them, joined together in the state elections of the non-

---

[15] Hicks, *Populist Revolt*, 241 ff. Stuart Noblin, *Leonidas LaFayette Polk: Agrarian Crusader* (Chapel Hill, N.C., 1949), is the best account of the Alliance in North Carolina down to Polk's death.

presidential year and swept to an astonishing victory that gave them safe majorities in both houses of the legislature. In other states the Populists in 1894 were not generally so successful as in North Carolina. But the election of a Populist governor in Nebraska, other scattered victories, and a sharp increase across the nation in the total Populist vote cast encouraged the party leaders. Most important, the acute economic stagnation after the panic of 1893 and President Cleveland's unyieldingly conservative policies led to astonishing defeats for the Democratic party throughout the country. True, the Republicans were the prime beneficiaries in 1894 from the increased unpopularity of the Democrats. But Populists, looking ahead, saw the Democratic party gradually disappearing, as had other major parties in American history, and the People's party emerging as the great national party of reform and the rival of the Republicans. Marion Butler was only one of many Populist spokesmen who envisioned such a bright future for the new party.[16]

Butler's immediate reward for his generalship in the campaign that brought the Tarheel Democrats their first statewide defeat since Reconstruction was a seat in the United States Senate. There he promptly proceeded to shock the veteran members by his vigorous advocacy of reform and to take his place alongside other agrarian champions of the silver cause. A journalist described the youthful senator as "a tall, broad shouldered, rather angular man, who swings down the street with that long stride that seems typical of his political career." In addition to a head of thick, dark hair, he wore a full but neatly trimmed beard, and as he talked he was said to narrow his deep-set, piercing eyes.[17] His youth probably inspired him

16 Hugh T. Lefler and Albert R. Newsome, *North Carolina: The History of a Southern State* (Chapel Hill, N.C., 1963), 507-17; Hicks, *Populist Revolt*, 321-39.

17 Carl Snyder, "Marion Butler," *Review of Reviews*, XIV (October 1896), 431-32.

not only to grow the beard but also to accentuate, whether consciously or unconsciously, another of his characteristics: his utter seriousness and lack of humor. Richly experienced for his age, he had come from a poverty-stricken state and class where politics was intense and, at times, downright dangerous business. It was certainly not in any relaxed or detached mood that the new senator from North Carolina set about attacking the Cleveland administration, defending the income tax, and above all clamoring for financial reform. With all of his power, he declared in the spring of 1895, he hoped to help make the financial question "the one over-shadowing issue in the next great struggle between the classes and the masses."[18]

Unlike some of the Western Populists, however, Butler disapproved of obliterating other demands in order to emphasize the silver issue. He admitted that government ownership of the railways was not widely popular but insisted that no great reform was ever popular at first. He thought that the correct solution of the railway problem was almost as important as that of the financial question. But the depression and money shortage had awakened the public to the silver issue and made the time ripe "for concentrating under one banner" those who supported reform. After winning the silver victory, Butler concluded, "I shall favor making a war to the finish on the greedy, grasping, private monopolies, which to-day are using and abusing the great functions of govern-

[18] Butler to D. H. Gill, May 2, 1895, in Butler's weekly newspaper, the Raleigh *Caucasian*, May 16, 1895. Despite its name the *Caucasian*, which Butler had purchased from a Democrat in the late 1880's, defended the Negro and deplored the political use of the race question. For example, the Populist paper pointed out that the "talk of 'nigger' and 'white rule' is already being started again in North Carolina for campaign purposes." The cry, so absurd when only about a quarter of North Carolina's population was Negro, had been used for years to hide election frauds and "goldbuggism." "What the great masses of the colored people in North Carolina want is fair treatment and justice and this they ought to have." *Ibid.*, March 12, 1896.

ment that should be owned by the people and used by the people."[19]

In short, what Butler and many other Populist leaders across the nation thought they had found by 1894-1895 was the common denominator that is essential in the life of a major political party in the United States. State and sectional groupings that differed widely because of differences in history and in economic interests might, with the right and lucky denominator, join together to win national victory. Doctrinaires and dogmatists saw the matter differently, but most of the Populist leaders were politicians who hoped to ride the financial issue to that first victory.[20]

Hindsight adds to the difficulty of understanding why such Populist leaders as Butler, along with numerous others, proceeded so confidently. The truth was that most of the Populist leaders, as well as large numbers of Republicans and Democrats, expected both of the old parties either to reject free silver outright or to equivocate. Either way, the Populists knew that their party stood to gain, for thousands of members

[19] Butler to Gill, *ibid.*, May 16, 1895. When the members of the supreme council of the Farmers' Alliance met in Raleigh to dedicate a monument to the late Colonel L. L. Polk, they had issued an address stating that while they stood firmly by all of the Alliance demands they recognized that no other reform was possible until "the destructive policy of contracting our money volume is overthrown, and the banks of the country be forced to retire from government business." Since the Alliance's demand for government ownership of all railways had long been a source of disagreement, the council proposed that the demand be changed to one for government ownership of just enough of competing railway lines to give the government effective control of all rate regulations. *Ibid.*, February 14, 1895. The Alliance, in other words, had hit on what a later generation would know as the "yardstick principle" in connection with the Tennessee Valley Authority and power rates.

[20] James A. Barnes, "Myths of the Bryan Campaign," *Mississippi Valley Historical Review*, XXXIV (December 1947), 369, makes virtually the same point: "Silver was but a symbol of things deep and fundamental, and its wisdom can be denied without lessening the significance of the revolt that Bryan led."

of the old parties were in no mood for the stale, ritualistic discussion of the tariff.

Senator Henry M. Teller of Colorado and other western Republicans were staunch friends of silver, but they were clearly a small minority in their business-minded party. Among the Democrats, such different leaders as Senator Ben Tillman of South Carolina and Governor John P. Altgeld of Illinois had joined the rebellion against Cleveland and were as clamorous for currency reform as any Populist. In the South and West the prosilver Democrats grew more numerous and vocal throughout 1895, but the extent of the rebellion against Cleveland and gold would not be clear until the late spring of 1896.[21]

Comforting to the Populists was the fact that the Democratic convention would meet under long-standing rules that required a vote of two-thirds of the delegates to name a presidential candidate. The Populists thought it almost certain that the Cleveland administration, with its power over patronage and the other resources of the executive branch, would have sufficient support from eastern delegates to block the nomination of an unequivocal friend of reform. A year before the Democratic convention met, Harry Skinner, Populist congressman from North Carolina, pointed to the two-thirds rule of the Democrats as the sure guarantee that the true friends of silver would have no recourse save to become Populists.[22]

The Populists said a great deal about "putting principle above party." Since most of them had walked out of the old parties when economic circumstances had become unbearable, their political righteousness had a certain legitimacy. To

[21] Harvey Wish, "John Peter Altgeld and the Background of the Campaign of 1896," *Mississippi Valley Historical Review*, XXIV (March 1938), 503-18.
[22] Skinner in the Washington *Post*, reprinted in the Raleigh *Caucasian*, June 27, 1895.

become a third-party man was not easy in most parts of the
nation, and in the South especially the break from tradition
required psychological daring and even physical courage. By
1895-1896, however, the Populist party was an important
institution. In it many persons had vital interests, interests
that were partly selfish where offices were concerned and
partly a reflection of genuine concern for a large mass of
suffering Americans. The two-thirds rule of the Democrats
made it vastly easier for General James B. Weaver, the
Populist presidential candidate in 1892, Chairman Taubeneck,
Senators Butler and Allen, and others to continue to insist
on the necessity of putting the silver principle above party
and to call and work in a variety of ways for a union of all the
silver forces in 1896.

Two minority factions within the People's party, for quite
different reasons, expressed misgivings about the silver-first
strategy and the constant calling for cooperative action of all
the friends of silver. The socialist followers of Lloyd, while
numerically small and unrepresentative, derived their significance from the brilliance and literary skill of Lloyd himself.
The other minority was much larger and consisted principally
of Populists in the South, especially the deep South, who,
for sectional reasons, disliked the idea of any cooperation
between Populists and Democrats.

Since real Republican organizations scarcely existed in some
of these southern states, Populists standing alone had to
contend with the high-handed and often dishonest machina-
tions of the long-entrenched Democrats. Not for silver, or
for that matter any other essentially national issue, were these
Populists willing to blur the distinction between themselves
and the Democrats. Opposing all fusion on principle, they
styled themselves "middle-of-the-road" Populists. As sincere
as most of them were in their Populism, the truth was that
they did not love the Populist party and its program more

than did the silver Populists—they only loved it differently and for different reasons.[23]

The first signs of the uneasiness of the "midroaders" in 1896 became evident in selecting a time for the Populist national convention. A Populist convention before either of the other two conventions would lessen the chances of co-operation or fusion, or cause the fusion, if any, to take place strictly on Populist terms with Populist candidates. The Populist national committee met in St. Louis on January 17 to decide when and where the convention would be held. The Republican committee had already scheduled their convention for St. Louis on June 16. The Democratic national committee met on January 16 and decided to hold their convention in Chicago on July 7.[24]

Marion Butler, like most of the national leaders of the party, favored a late convention. The Populist state chairman of Nebraska had urged, as early as August 1895, that the Populists hold their national convention after both of the old parties had "unquestionably turned their backs upon the white metal."[25]

On the other hand, from Thomson, Georgia, Watson's home, a Populist national committeeman sent Butler his proxy along with regrets that he could not be in St. Louis and expressed the hope that the committee would call the convention for early spring and meet in some Southern city,

[23] For Watson's warning, as early as 1892, through his *People's Party Paper* about the emphasis on silver, see Woodward, *Watson*, 278 ff.

[24] New York *Tribune*, January 17, 1896.

[25] J. H. Edmisten, of Lincoln, Nebraska, to Butler, August 14, 1895, Butler MSS. Later, on the eve of the national committee's meeting, Mann Page of Virginia and others wrote the same thing to Butler and sent him their proxies. Bryan himself, who was working mightily to swing the national Democratic party to silver, also urged Ignatius Donnelly to help persuade the Populists to meet late so that they could "take advantage of the errors of the old parties" and more easily "bring about a consolidation of all the silver forces." Bryan to Donnelly, January 1, 1896, in Paul W. Glad, *The Trumpet Soundeth: William Jennings Bryan and His Democracy, 1896-1912* (Lincoln, Nebr., 1960), 55.

preferably Atlanta.[26] The Populist national committee, apparently reflecting the sentiment of the majority of the party membership, decided to hold the convention in St. Louis on July 22, and invited all opponents of the two old parties to cooperate with the Populists.[27]

Counting on the Democrats' two-thirds rule to be the final making of the Populist party, Butler and the other leaders worked diligently for the silver cause throughout the spring of 1896. In the Senate Butler attacked the party-first Democrats and Republicans who claimed to be silverites. The Atlanta *Constitution* thought that he had secured "a hearing hardly ever given to a Populist" and "smoked out of the bushes men who have been playing a hide-and-seek game with their constituencies for years."[28]

In North Carolina an increasing number of Democratic leaders became converts to silver, sometimes from conviction and sometimes for expediency's sake. Despite this growing Democratic shift, Butler received encouraging signs for Populism too. A Negro voter wrote: "I am a colored man and a Republican and have been for seventeen years; but be it thoroughly understood that I am not married to any party that will dodge from justice to the people and yield to the few who want to enslave the country by a single gold standard law." He advised every Negro voter to take the *Caucasian* and "stop going around howling 'straight Republican ticket.'"[29]

[26] C. H. Ellington to Butler, January 3, 1896, Butler MSS. Hicks, *Populist Revolt*, 350, points out that Harry Tracy's *Southern Mercury* in Texas favored the early convention and said so emphatically and early. The *Mercury* was not, however, as representative of southern Populist opinion as Hicks implies. For Tracy, who owned the *Mercury*, and his even more extreme editor, Milton Park, see Roscoe C. Martin, *The People's Party in Texas* (Austin, 1933), 127-29, 246.

[27] New York *Tribune*, January 18, 1896.

[28] Quoted in the Raleigh *Caucasian*, January 9, 1896.

[29] *Ibid.*, March 5, 1896. For a similar letter from six Negroes who thought that a "little more of the 'stick to your party'" will put us in a worse condition than we were in the days of chat[t]el slavery," see *ibid.*, March 19, 1896.

A white Democrat, preparing to bolt to the Populists, wanted to know why it was not "more patriotic and wise" to bolt now than it had been for the Southern Democrats to bolt the national party in 1860. "The issue confronting the American people to-day is the liberty of the laboring people, both white and black," the Tarheel declared, "an issue of vastly more importance than the enslavement or freedom of the negro ever was." Nor had the depression abated to make the cry for reform less urgent. One old farmer reported: "If Miss Prosperity has made her appearance in this section, she certainly has appeared wrong end forward, for there never has been, since Adam was a boy, such weeping, wailing and gnashing of teeth known here among the poor."[30]

The Republican convention that opened on June 16 declared itself "unreservedly for sound money" and opposed to the free coinage of silver "except by international agreement with the leading commercial nations of the earth, which agreement we pledge ourselves to promote." The Republicans also equivocated on their candidate by naming William McKinley of Ohio, who preferred to talk about the beauties of the high tariff because he had in the past been friendly to silver. Senator Teller of Colorado, Senator Richard F. Pettigrew of South Dakota, and other silver Republicans from the far West bolted the party and announced their intention to organize the Silver Republican party.[31]

The plan of the Silver Republicans and the Populist leaders was to rally around Senator Teller as the ideal candidate for the united silver forces. He had favored the income tax and a few other reforms and had stood for years as one of the most widely respected spokesmen for silver. If the eastern friends of the Cleveland administration had the votes to force

[30] *Ibid.*, March 5, 12, 1896.
[31] Detailed studies on this development are Ellis, *Teller*, 255-64, and the same author's "The Silver Republicans in the Election of 1896," *Mississippi Valley Historical Review*, XVIII (March 1932), 519-34.

a compromise candidate on the Democratic convention, true silver Democrats by the thousands would come to the silver banner that would be primarily the property of the Populists. If, on the other hand, the admittedly powerful silver wing of the Democrats should be in control sufficiently to name the candidate as well as to write the platform, the Silver Republican and Populist leaders insisted that no candidate would be as acceptable as Teller if the silver Democrats were sincere about wanting to unite all the silver forces. Taubeneck, Butler, Pettigrew, Senator Fred Dubois of Idaho, Senator William M. Stewart of Nevada, and others worked arduously for Teller to receive the Democratic nomination.[32]

But a veritable revolution had occurred in the Democratic party; its full extent could not be measured until the fervent silverites began to flock into Chicago for the convention on July 7. "The Democratic movement toward silver in the last six months before the Chicago convention," Professor Allan Nevins has written, "was like an avalanche: a mere whisper at first, than a half-imperceptible shift in the landscape, and suddenly a roar, a crash, an irresistible cataclysm."[33]

Cleveland's last hopes for blocking the nomination of a genuine reformer were pinned on William C. Whitney, his millionaire adviser and former secretary of the navy. Whitney loaded up his "special train of three handsome parlor cars"

[32] Ellis, *Teller,* 261 ff. A key source for the plan to secure Teller's nomination is the correspondence of Butler to Stewart in late June and early July 1896, in the William M. Stewart MSS, Nevada State Historical Society. Photostats of these letters were kindly furnished the author by Professor H. Wayne Morgan; the letters are also reproduced in Effie M. Mack, "Life and Letters of William Morris Stewart, 1827-1909," unpublished dissertation at the University of California (1930), 267-71.

[33] Nevins, *Grover Cleveland: A Study in Courage* (New York, 1934), 689. For a recent study that is more sympathetic to Bryan, see Paolo E. Coletta, "Bryan, Cleveland, and the Disrupted Democracy, 1890-1896," *Nebraska History,* XLI (March 1960), 1-27. J. Rogers Hollingsworth, *The Whirligig of Politics: The Democracy of Cleveland and Bryan* (Chicago, 1963), is helpful on the Democrats but wrong about the Populist convention of 1896.

with loyal eastern followers of Cleveland and headed for Chicago. Upon arrival there one of these Cleveland Democrats left the special train, with its ample supply of "comestibles and drinkables," to mingle with his assembled fellow-Democrats. He soon reported to Whitney, "For the first time I can understand the scenes of the French Revolution."[34]

The jubilant and determined silver Democrats, in easy control of the proceedings as soon as the convention opened, did want to unite the various reform parties but to antagonize as few conservative Democrats as possible in the process. Consequently, they rejected Teller despite all the pressure that the Populists and Silver Republicans could exert. Teller himself had never believed it possible that the Democrats would nominate him, and his repeated public statements that such an action on their part might be "injudicious" added to the difficulty of his supporters' task. Teller also announced that he would give his support to any one of several prominent silver Democrats.

More important, leading silver Democrats, especially Altgeld, realized that silverite control of the convention would mean a bolt from the party by eastern followers of Cleveland, a more serious and sizable bolt than the silverites had inflicted upon the Republican party. The nomination of Teller would only aggravate the problem of holding as many Democrats as possible in the party. Altgeld's public statement the day the convention opened that he doubted if Teller could carry Illinois was a major setback for the Teller boom.

Populist Chairman Taubeneck's public statement that the Populists would not support such partisan Democrats as Congressman Richard P. ("Silver Dick") Bland of Missouri or Governor Horace Boies of Iowa was one factor that worked

---

[34] Nevins, *Cleveland*, 700. Horace S. Merrill, *Bourbon Leader: Grover Cleveland and the Democratic Party* (Boston, 1957), 182 ff., is useful on the conservative Democrats.

against those two leading contenders for the nomination. This situation together with William Jennings Bryan's careful preconvention work for support among the delegates, his outstanding record in Congress as an able friend of reform, his clear record of friendliness to and cooperation with the Populists in his home state, and, lastly, his magnetic qualities as displayed in his famed address to the convention led to the young Nebraskan's nomination by the Democrats.[35]

Not only had the Democrats named the most exciting and dynamic presidential candidate in well over a generation but the platform, in addition to the call for free silver and other financial reforms, bore the stamp of Governor Altgeld in its denunciation of Cleveland's action in the Pullman boycott and of "government by injunction as a new and highly dangerous form of oppression." Too often remembered only for its assaults on the "anti-American," "British policy" of gold monometallism, the Democratic platform also demanded stricter federal regulation of the railways, an end to national banknotes, a tariff for revenue only (after the money question was settled), an income tax, the protection of American labor by prevention of the "importation of foreign pauper labor," stricter enforcement of antitrust legislation, and various other reforms.[36] For all the Populists who since the party's birth had cried "principle above party" a cruel moment of decision had arrived.

National history made it clear by 1896 that an important

[35] Ellis, *Teller*, 267-73. Bryan himself said later in *The First Battle: A Story of the Campaign of 1896* (Chicago, 1896), 296-97, that he believed his nomination could be "attributed more to the friendly relations existing between Democrats, Populists, and silver Republicans than to any other one cause." A prescient Nebraska Populist had written General Weaver long before the national conventions that Bryan was "practically a Populist, except in name." Furthermore: "He can carry the solid south. No Populist can do that—and we *must have* the solid south." J. Burrows to Weaver, May, 1896, as quoted in Silveus, "The Antecedents of the Campaign of 1896," 211-12.

[36] The document is reprinted in Bryan, *First Battle*, 406-409.

third party faced one of two fates: it died after growing strong enough to force one of the major parties to embrace its ideas and the bulk of its membership, or, given the right set of circumstances, it might become in a time of general party disintegration and chaos one of the two major parties. The Democrats in 1896, however, had not equivocated and dodged in the face of an overwhelming national question as the Whigs had tried to do in the decade before the Civil War.

Although no Populist planned or wished the party's death, the western Populists could accept the possibility of this national fate for the party with a certain equanimity and a redoubled resolve to work for Bryan, silver, and then other reforms. Populists in many western states had early begun the practice of cooperating or "fusing" with Democrats in political battles against Republicans, who were dominant in the West. In 1892, in fact, the Democrats, who were almost as weak in some of the western states as the Republicans were in the South, had helped to elect Grover Cleveland to his second term by voting for the Populists' presidential candidate, General James B. Weaver. Seeing that their only chance of keeping a number of the western states out of the Republican electoral column was through support for Weaver, thousands of Democrats in Kansas, Nebraska, the Dakotas, and other western states voted for the Populist electoral tickets and helped the third party to win twenty-two electoral votes, an impressive achievement for the national debut of a new political party in the United States.

Nor were the Populists the only beneficiaries of this cooperative politics in the West. Democratic candidates on state and congressional tickets frequently received endorsement by the Populists. Bryan, for example, shared many of the reformist views of the Populists, and they had helped reelect him to Congress from Nebraska in 1892. Given this background, western Populists could hardly be shocked by the possibility of Populist cooperation with, and possible absorption on the national scene by, the revitalized Democratic party of 1896.[37]

To the southern Populist, however, absorption by the Democrats was a fate too unspeakable to be contemplated. No matter what the historic pattern concerning third parties or the logic of the national situation might be, sectional exigencies in the South demanded the preservation of a separate and distinct Populist party. The situation that faced the Populists after the Democratic convention in Chicago, therefore, seemed to be this: if the Populists did not fall in line behind Bryan and free silver, the bulk of the western strength of the party would be lost as Populists there left the party to march under the Democratic banner of reform. If the Populists did nominate Bryan, and run the risk of having the Democrats swallow the third party on the national level, the southern Populists to save their local political lives and for largely sectional reasons would be sorely tempted to bolt the national Populist party.

Either way, in the short interval between the conclusion of the Democratic convention and the opening of the Populist meeting in St. Louis on July 22, the split between the pro-Bryan Populists and the southern midroaders seemed to augur the certain dissolution of the People's party.

[37] Hicks, *Populist Revolt*, 255-62. During the campaign of 1896, Senator Charles J. Faulkner, chairman of the Democratic congressional campaign, explained the reasons for the Democratic support of the Populist national ticket in many western states in 1892 and declared that "whatever Mr. Bryan or any other Democrat did in the support of Weaver was at the request of the National Democratic committee." New York *Times*, September 25, 1896; Raleigh *News and Observer*, September 27, 1896.

2

The St. Louis Convention

Several prominent western Populists announced shortly after Bryan's nomination that they favored Populist endorsement of the Democratic national ticket. Butler, Taubeneck, and some of the Silver Republican leaders, however, still favored Senator Teller as the candidate for the Populists and for the National Silver party, whose convention was also to begin in St. Louis on July 22. Butler's newspaper continued to attack the Democratic party on the state and national levels, though the Tarheel Populist leader carefully refrained from attacking Bryan himself.

As Butler saw the situation on the eve of the Populist convention and described his views to Senator Stewart, there were two courses open to the Populists. They could endorse Bryan under certain conditions or they could name their own candidates, with the understanding that after the election the presidential electors would use every honorable effort to combine the votes of all electors who favored silver and opposed the rule of the national banks. Butler added that he preferred the latter course, which would certainly simplify matters for the southern Populists, and believed that it was not only necessary but the most promising plan for good results. But he did not favor publicity for either of the plans until the Populist convention had actually begun.[1]

Teller was not available for the Populist-National Silver nomination for the simple reason that he supported the

Democratic ticket and insisted that all the silver forces should do the same. After writing his Republican friends as well as Butler, Taubeneck, and other Populists to this effect, Teller informed Bryan: "I have written to all the Populist leaders that I know and some that I do not urging them to nominate you and I made it impossible for my name to be used."[2]

Butler's own conversion to the idea of accepting Bryan was facilitated by the advice he received from Senator Stewart, who had attended the Democratic convention. The Nevadan informed Butler that the Democrats who controlled the Chicago convention "were as emphatically Populists in their sentiments and actions as yourself" and that the "platform is radical enough for you or me." Since Bryan was "more of a Populist than a Democrat," Stewart continued, the western Populists were emphatically for him. Any attempt to run an opposing candidate would not only fail but destroy the party. Stewart insisted: "There is no use fighting the movement now. We must join with it or be destroyed. There was nothing left of the Democratic party at Chicago but the name."[3]

Since the Populist response even to the name "Democrat" differed greatly according to sectional circumstances, confusion and anxiety mounted as the Populists began to converge on St. Louis. Reporters found that some delegates, too poor to pay railway fares, had walked long distances to reach the convention. Some were forced to sleep in the parks in order to afford the "nickel-lunch." Heat gripped the city. Eastern newsmen, like their publishers and editors, were apt to be

[1] Photostat of Butler to Stewart, July 13, 1896, Stewart MSS. Also the Raleigh *Caucasian*, July 16, 1896. For Pettigrew's plea to Teller on July 10, begging him not to endorse Bryan so that the Populists and National Silver party could nominate Teller at St. Louis and "after McKinley is beaten unite our electors on some man for President," see Ellis, "The Silver Republicans in the Election of 1896," 531.

[2] Teller to Bryan, July 18, 1896, Bryan MSS, Library of Congress.

[3] Stewart to Butler, July 14, 1896, as cited in Mack, "Life and Letters of Stewart," 272-73.

intolerant of the desperate farmers. The correspondent for the New York *Times* wrote: "The crazy people who fancy that some one is always sneaking paris green into their chowder or needles into their hash are not more suspicious than this body of 1,400 more or less 'touched' would-be rulers of the country."[4]

Marion Butler refused interviews and kept quiet as he had said he would, but few other Populist leaders chose that course. Captain Reuben F. Kolb, prominent leader of the Alabama delegation, declared strongly for Bryan: "I am willing to make the fight on one plank, so long as it is monetary reform. That is the paramount issue. I'm a middle-of-the-road Populist, but I've got sense enough to walk around a mud hole." From Texas, where anti-Bryan and midroad sentiment was strongest, a delegate asserted that a straight Populist ticket would be named because "Texas is going to run this convention and dictate the nominations." Although Tom Watson had chosen not to attend the convention, he had dispatched the Georgia delegation with instructions to stand by the full Populist platform and fight fusion with the Democrats.[5]

At the other extreme from Watson and the Texans, most western Populists were loud in their praises for the Democratic candidates and platform. Representative Jerry Simpson of Kansas told the large and generally approving Kansas delegation that the "issue is paramount, and men dare not play politics at such a time as this. If this Convention should refuse to indorse Bryan the Populist party would not contain a corporal's guard in November."[6]

[4] New York *Times*, July 25, 1896.

[5] St. Louis *Globe-Democrat*, July 21, 1896, has the quotations and identifies the Texan delegate as Judge Lee M. Callaway of Corsicana; Woodward, *Watson*, 293.

[6] St. Louis *Globe-Democrat*, July 21, 1896. Hicks, *Populist Revolt*, 357, describes and quotes Simpson's views and adds this sentence: "So also

Out of this babel a plan emerged. The party not only made nominations but was also largely held together. Leadership, bold and imaginative as the difficult situation required, played a key role. The fundamental fact was that most Populists wanted free silver as the first step and symbol of overdue reforms. Most Populists wanted also to maintain their party organization intact for the national purpose of keeping the Democrats "honest" and out of the hands of Cleveland men and for various local purposes that differed according to geography and circumstance. Henry D. Lloyd's widely accepted charge that the Populist leaders at St. Louis "tricked and bulldozed and betrayed" as they carried out a program to destroy Populism is not only untrue but also ignores the dilemma that faced the party.[7]

No one can say with assurance who first suggested that the Populists should nominate Bryan, reject the Democrats' vice-presidential nominee, Arthur Sewall of Maine, and put up their own candidate for the vice-presidency. Senator Marion Butler, however, carefully considered the plan and its complications before arriving in St. Louis, and he early and energetically identified himself with this method of saving both the Populist party and the unity of the silver forces. As unprecedented and fraught with difficulty as the plan was, it alone seemed to meet the complexities of the party situation

---

thought Weaver and Allen and a host of minor lights, some of whom had an eye on the loaves and fishes." This impugning of the motives of the Populists who supported Bryan is hardly fair. The argument could also be made, though it should not be, that southern midroaders feared fusion with Democrats because their local offices would be jeopardized by such a program. The correspondent for the Democratic Atlanta *Constitution*, for example, charged on July 23, 1896, that the "whole fight of every 'middle of the road' man is for the possession of office, to get some one in a snug berth."

[7] Lloyd to A. B. Adair, October 10, 1896, Lloyd MSS. Lloyd's important article, "The Populists at St. Louis," *Review of Reviews*, XIV (September 1896), 298-303, is more sympathetic toward the action of the convention than his private comments at the time, although the article too is misleading.

that the executive committeemen faced when they gathered in St. Louis on Sunday evening, July 19. And this was the plan that was ultimately accepted by the great majority both of the leaders and of the ordinary delegates who filled the hotel lobbies with noisy, often angry debate.[8]

Butler arrived with the reputation of being a midroader who opposed fusion with the Democrats. He was and continued to be a moderate one in the sense that he, Taubeneck, Senator William A. Peffer of Kansas, and others in the majority agreed that the national organization of the Populist party should be preserved. It should neither be destroyed by a bolt of the extreme fusionists from the West, who favored endorsement of both Bryan and Sewall, or by the extreme midroaders of the deep South, who insisted on a straight Populist ticket, nor should the party be eliminated by being absorbed in the Democracy. This sentiment the executive committee established at its first meeting.[9]

Senator James K. Jones of Arkansas, the Democratic national chairman, and Governor William J. Stone, Democrat of Missouri, met with the Populist leaders and insisted on

[8] For evidence that Butler had a North Carolinian in mind for the Populist vice-presidential nomination, possibly Walter Clark, an associate justice of the North Carolina Supreme Court, see W. J. Peele to Butler, July 18, 20, 1896, Butler MSS. In addition to other newspapermen who pointed to Butler as the foremost architect of the convention's work, Josephus Daniels, who was no friend of Butler's, attended the convention and reported to his newspaper: "Butler is being praised and blamed as the author of the plan. It was born out of the necessities of the situation. Butler saw what other leaders might have seen, and what newspaper men saw. It may truly be said that the policy pursued prevented a bolt." Raleigh *News and Observer*, July 28, 1896. See also Carl Snyder, "Marion Butler," *Review of Reviews*, XIV (October 1896), 429-33. Even Lloyd, in "The Populists at St. Louis," 298, declared that one of the best representatives of the convention was Butler, "the handsome young farmer of North Carolina" who was "too young to be a candidate" but had "worked his way up from his fields through the Farmers' Alliance into a seat in the United States Senate."

[9] St. Louis *Globe-Democrat*, July 20, 1896; St. Louis *Republic*, July 20, 1896. Since no official record of the Populist convention was ever published, the historian must rely largely on contemporary accounts in the newspapers—and be accordingly alert for the difference between fact and rumor.

full endorsement of the Democratic ticket or nothing. Bryan's spokesmen emphatically rejected, as did the western Populists, the idea that Butler and others presented of an independent Populist ticket with Populist candidates, to be followed by fusion with the other silver groups on the electoral ticket according to the proportionate strength of the various parties in each state. One alleged spokesman for Bryan, Matt Ward of Omaha, Nebraska, declared flatly that, "This talk about dividing electors will not be allowed; it can't go. I have Mr. Bryan's ultimatum in my pocket, and will deliver it to the Populists at the proper time."[10]

Butler had discovered, even before arriving in St. Louis, that while it was both difficult and impolitic to attack Bryan himself, the same was not true of the Democratic vice-presidential nominee. Arthur Sewall was a well-to-do shipbuilder who had, at one time or other, been connected with a national bank and with railway and other corporations. He also believed in free silver and was nominated because he was from Maine and would furnish a sectional balance for a ticket headed by a Nebraskan. Any hope that his eastern "respectability" would help hold irate Cleveland Democrats in the party proved futile.

The most enthusiastic Democrat knew that Bryan had about the same chance in New England as McKinley had in the deep South. Both the extremist minority of midroad Populists, who were ready to split the party rather than accept Bryan, and the more moderate leaders, who searched for a way to save the party and the silver cause, announced that Sewall could never be accepted by the Populists.[11]

Capitalizing on this anti-Sewall feeling, Butler conferred

[10] St. Louis *Globe-Democrat*, July 20, 1896.

[11] For Butler's initial hostility to Sewall, see Raleigh *Caucasian*, July 16, 1896; for the same sentiment among a larger group of Populist editors in the Reform Press Association which met in St. Louis on the eve of the Populist convention, see St. Louis *Globe-Democrat*, July 20, 1896.

again with Senator Jones on Monday, July 20, and proposed, according to apparently reliable press accounts, that the Populists endorse Bryan if the Democrats would drop Sewall and accept the Populist nominee for vice president. When Jones refused to listen to this proposal, Butler reportedly became angry and assailed the Democrats for "wanting the earth." Butler's later statement to newsmen revealed little other than his hope for a way out: "Some seem to think that there is a danger of a split, but there will be none. The different elements will put their heads together and agree on a plan of action."[12]

Just as Jones rebuffed Butler, Weaver and other spokesmen for the complete Bryan-Sewall ticket rejected the same proposition when James H. ("Cyclone") Davis of Texas and Ignatius Donnelly of Minnesota presented it on behalf of the Populist executive committee. Any attempt to displace Sewall, according to Jones and his allies, would lead to irreconcilable complications and place both parties in a ridiculous attitude. "The committee," Jones declared, "must be as loyal to the vice presidential nominee as to the presidential candidate."[13]

In spite of Jones's refusal to talk about a sacrifice of Sewall, a key group of Populist leaders, including Marion Butler, had decided by Tuesday, July 21, the day before the convention opened, that the exigencies of the situation called for the nomination of Bryan and a southern Populist on a Populist ticket backed by a Populist platform. But this program would have to be fought for in open convention,

[12] St. Louis *Globe-Democrat*, July 21, 1896.
[13] *Ibid.* Jones also attempted to block the movement to ignore Sewall by promising that Populist endorsement of the Democratic ticket would be followed by his naming two or three Populists to the executive committee that would manage Bryan's campaign. New York *Herald*, July 21, and St. Louis *Globe-Democrat*, July 22, 1896. The *Herald* reporter mixed all sorts of rumors designed to discredit Jones and the Democrats in his detailed stories.

where a slight misstep might see minorities on either extreme
ganging up to thwart what seemed to be the complicated
preference of the majority.

When the Populist national committee met on July 21,
the executive committee, which had met earlier, recommended and secured Marion Butler's nomination as the
temporary chairman and keynote speaker of the convention.
Although "Cyclone" Davis of Texas and General Weaver of
Kansas had been frequently mentioned by their respective
factions for the temporary chairmanship, opposition to Butler
scarcely materialized either in the meeting of the national
committee or in the convention itself.[14]

The convention that finally opened on Wednesday, July
22, consisted of almost 1,400 hot, confused, and tense delegates. Palmetto fans agitated the stagnant air. The audibility
of the speakers on the platform was so poor that a big-voiced
delegate from Wisconsin had to be used as a "repeater." A
few women and Negro delegates were scattered about the hall.
Each state was allowed one delegate for every senator and
representative it had in Congress and additional delegates in
proportion to the Populist vote cast in the state. This plan

[14] St. Louis *Republic,* July 20, 1896; Raleigh *News and Observer,* July 22,
1896. The latter account describes how the Bryan-Sewall committeemen
decided to put up General James G. Field of Virginia rather than Weaver
for the temporary chairmanship and then withdrew Field to allow Butler to
be nominated by acclamation. The *Globe-Democrat,* July 22, reports that a
caucus of the extreme midroaders, led by Texans, was meeting when the news
came of Butler's nomination as temporary chairman; Harry Tracy and two
others were sent to invite Butler to address the caucus. Tracy returned to
report that, "Senator Butler told me he was in favor of adopting a Populist
platform and tendering the nomination to Bryan." Although hisses greeted
this news, Davis defended Butler and Jerome C. Kearby, another Texas
leader, refused to allow his name to be entered against Butler's. The caucus
finally fixed on an obscure Missourian to run against Butler for the temporary
chairmanship, as the Silver Democrats had revolted against Senator David Hill
of New York at their Chicago convention. But the next day when the
convention actually began the Texans decided not to make the fight—
obviously because such extreme midroadism was in a small minority.

of representation meant that New York had only forty-four delegates, based mostly on population, while Texas and North Carolina each had around a hundred votes, and Kansas, with the largest western delegation, had eighty-two. One analysis of the convention by sections showed that the South had about six hundred delegates, or nearly half; the East, one hundred and fifty; the North (including Ohio and to the Missouri river but not including Missouri and the Dakotas), two hundred and forty; and the West (beyond the Missouri), three hundred and fifty-six.[15]

With extremists on both sides waiting for their openings to yell in uninhibited Populist style, Butler successfully walked an oratorical tightrope in his keynote address. He suggested that the Democrats, from a mixture of alarm and conscience, had committed "petty and grand larceny by stealing the People's party platform almost in its entirety." What then should the Populists do? They should insist upon putting issues above partisanship, as they had traditionally demanded, and help settle the financial question so that other fundamental matters could be dealt with next.

But the separate People's party was still absolutely necessary. Without it, "the next Democratic National Convention would repudiate the platform it recently adopted at Chicago, and Mr. Bryan would stand no more chance four years hence of being nominated by that party than Thomas Jefferson would if he were alive." Without alluding directly to the plan for a southern vice-presidential nominee, Butler con-

[15] New York *Herald*, July 19, 1896. Silveus, "The Antecedents of the Campaign of 1896," 110, gives the number of delegates that each state was assigned by the national committee's original call for the convention. When Texas and some other southern states complained, however, the national committee granted them increases in voting strength—in the case of Texas from 95 to 103 delegates. The statement in Hicks, *Populist Revolt*, 361, that the plan of representation favored the West at the expense of the South is based on Tracy's charge in the *Southern Mercury*, February 27, 1896, and does not appear to be correct about the final composition of the convention.

cluded with a plea for unity, which, under the circumstances, was hardly mere rhetoric. A party that had raised up a great principle and split the two old parties, he argued, "is not going to be foolish enough to allow itself to split on methods and detail. We will stand together."[16]

After the keynote address the convention adjourned until evening to give the committee on permanent organization time to prepare its report. Since there had been no floor fight about Butler's election, all hands prepared for battle about the election of the permanent chairman of the convention. The extreme midroaders filled the air with their threats of bolting if the leaders tried to force the nomination of Bryan. The election of the permanent chairman, as all declared at the time, would be the first test of the power of the various factions.

When the delegates reassembled at 8 P.M. they found the convention hall in darkness. A few candles at the press table cast a weird light as the band played bravely and some of the restless delegates tried to sing. Some of the extreme midroaders concluded that the darkness had resulted from a trick of the Bryan men. Someone yelled, "Its a scheme of the Bryan men" and if "they" nominate Bryan "we'll split this convention." "You're a disgrace to the party," came back from the dark depths of the hall. One delegate from Texas, a congressional candidate, declared, "There has been some ugly work, and the culprits had better beware."[17]

After the aisles began to choke with pushing and shouting delegates, Davis of Texas finally got the attention of the

[16] Bryan, *First Battle*, 259-64, reprints the text. The New York *Herald*, July 23, 1896, reported that Butler's "adroit" speech made such a strong impression that many delegates were mentioning him for the vice-presidential nomination. His age, however, would have made that constitutionally impossible, since he was only thirty-three.

[17] Raleigh *Caucasian*, July 30, 1896, has many of these details in a firsthand account that was probably written by the editor, Hal Ayer, who was also a delegate to the convention; see also St. Louis *Globe-Democrat*, July 23, 1896, and Raleigh *News and Observer*, July 24, 1896.

crowd: "As his tall form and broad, sweeping sombrero came within the narrow ring of light from the tallow dip, the delegates immediately recognized him, and there were shouts of 'shut up,' 'keep quiet,' 'Listen to Cyclone.' " He yelled that the "electric wires were 'disaffected' " but would be repaired soon. Nevertheless, at 8:45 P.M. Butler, probably fearing greater chaos in the darkness, announced that the accident in the lighting would prevent the committees from reporting that night and declared the convention recessed until the following morning.[18]

This episode is important both because it illustrates the mood of certain elements of the convention and because it has been cited by various historians as a mysterious development that Butler and other "manipulators" may really have been responsible for, a part of the "conspiracy" for Bryan at St. Louis. The simple truth was that the heat in St. Louis, which had reached a point that inspired editorial comment, exploded about 6 P.M. in a rain and electrical storm that knocked down some power lines.[19]

Regardless of the lights, those delegates who would proceed with passionate disregard of the danger of splitting the party were in a minority. Certainly the voting on the permanent chairmanship proved that the next day (Thursday, July 23). The majority report of the committee on permanent organization recommended Senator William Allen of Nebraska, a fervent supporter of Bryan who was also believed by most observers to favor Sewall. The minority report named James

[18] Raleigh *Caucasian*, July 30, 1896; St. Louis *Globe-Democrat*, July 23, 1896.

[19] St. Louis *Globe-Democrat*, July 23, 1896; Raleigh *News and Observer*, July 23, 1896. The correspondent of the Atlanta *Constitution*, July 23, 1896, referred to a "terrific cyclone" that hit the city as night fell. After quoting the editor of the *Southern Mercury* about the "fusion gang's" plunging the hall into darkness to confound the midroaders, Hicks, *Populist Revolt*, 361, states: "Whatever the situation might have been had the lights not gone out, next morning the fusionists were clearly in the majority." For later and continuing charges by Texans about a pro-Bryan plot in connection with the episode, see Martin, *People's Party in Texas*, 241.

E. Campion, an obscure extreme midroader from Maine. Allen was chosen, 758 to 564.

Thus a majority of the convention agreed on a Bryan man for permanent chairman. An even larger majority later accepted the report of the committee on the platform as made by General Weaver and rejected proposals backed by some of the extremists led by Coxey of Ohio. The platform recognized the financial question as the "great and pressing issue" before the country, and Populists invited the "co-operation of all organizations and citizens" who agreed on "this vital question."

In addition to the important cluster of demands dealing with finance, the Populists joined the new Democracy in calling for an income tax, an end to the misuse of the injunction in labor disputes, and other reforms. The Populists still included several of their usual demands which the Democrats had not espoused, such as government ownership of the railroads and telegraph, reclamation by the Federal government of lands granted to the railroads and other corporations in "excess of their actual needs"; direct legislation through the initiative and referendum; the election of the president, vice president, and senators by a "direct vote of the people"; and jobs on public works for the unemployed in times of industrial depression. The platform, in short, represented the majority's desire to express the independence of the Populists as well as to invite cooperation with other reform forces on the paramount issue.[20]

The undecided, crucial question remained: would the extreme midroaders bolt, as they constantly threatened, after the majority named Bryan as the Populist candidate? The extreme fusionists, who insisted that the Populists had to

[20] The platform is reprinted in Bryan, *First Battle*, 271-76; the New York *Herald*, July 25, 1896, reports its adoption. The Populist platform also denounced "the wholesale system of disfranchisement" that Mississippi and South Carolina had already adopted.

accept Sewall as well as Bryan, were counting on either a stampede to Sewall in the enthusiastic aftermath of Bryan's nomination or an adjournment after that nomination to give them time to woo a majority to Sewall. If the Southern extremists bolted, moreover, the task of selling Sewall to the delegates remaining in the convention would become that much easier.[21]

In order to prevent any possibility of Sewall's being nominated, the minority report of the committee on rules and procedures called for a reversal of the usual order of nominations and the naming of the vice-presidential candidate first. Texans, Georgians, and others rallied to this idea, not only because they were anti-Sewall but also because they hoped that somehow the presidential nomination might be miraculously saved for a Populist too. The next round of voting began.

North Carolina, which had divided its ninety-five votes equally in the Allen-Campion contest for the permanent chairmanship, was a key state in the tense fight about the order of business. When the roll call reached it, Congressman Harry Skinner mounted a chair and shouted: "North Carolina stands with Nebraska. When we came here this morning we were for the minority report, but since then we have had assurances from Kansas, Nebraska, and other . . . States that, if we would permit the regular order to prevail the cause of Populism in the South should be recognized by the nomination of a Southern candidate for Vice-President. North Carolina therefore casts 85 votes for the majority report and 10 for the minority."

As the roll call neared the end, rumors began to circulate that the Bryanites had narrowly won with the majority report

---

[21] The National Silver party also began its convention in St. Louis on July 22 but had little influence on the Populists. After nominating Bryan and Sewall on Friday, July 24, the Silver party adjourned without waiting for the Populist nominations.

for the traditional order of nominations. Southern midroaders rushed to beg the North Carolina delegation to change its vote. Skinner hurriedly consulted with Butler, rushed back to his delegation, and again mounted the chair: "Mr. Chairman, North Carolina cast its vote to nominate a President first, after pledges from Kansas and other States that afterwards a [southern] Populist should be nominated for Vice-President. Are you sincere? I demand to know as I am empowered to change the vote of North Carolina."

Bedlam descended upon the convention. Cries of "yes, yes" and "no" filled the air. Thomas Patterson, head of the Colorado delegation and a leading supporter for the Bryan-Sewall ticket, yelled that it was "disgraceful that in a convention like this any such deals should be mentioned." He vowed that "Colorado had no part in it."

Skinner, probably exhausting the patience of many with his further remarks about a southern man's deserving the vice-presidential nomination, concluded by casting all of North Carolina's ninety-five votes for the minority report. With the convention again in churning commotion and Marion Butler on the platform cheering "as long as his voice held out," Allen finally restored order to announce that the minority report had carried by 785 votes to 615. A Populist vice-presidential candidate would be named first.[22]

The midroaders, both the extreme and moderate ones cooperating, had won their first clear victory. They celebrated accordingly, the extremists temporarily ignoring the limited nature of their victory. The anti-Bryan midroaders hurt their own cause through lack of organization and noisy immoderation in general. One sympathetic observer remarked that the

[22] Raleigh *Caucasian*, July 30, 1896, has the most detailed account of this but see also St. Louis *Globe-Democrat*, July 25, 1896, St. Louis *Republic*, July 25, 1896, and Raleigh *News and Observer*, July 25, 1896. Some accounts give the final vote as 738 to 637, but in any case the point is clear that North Carolina's votes were necessary for the minority report on the order of business to win.

large Texas delegation was composed of some of the "best men on the American continent" but was handicapped, nevertheless, by such "wild fools as a man named Wilkins from California, and a high cheeked and peak headed yahoo from Missouri, and two or three other similar characters. These cranks put the many good men of the mid-road faction to disadvantage."[23]

Despite these handicaps, the midroaders came into their own at about sixteen minutes before 1 A.M. (the appropriateness of the "sixteen to one" amused them) on Saturday, July 25, when one of their best-loved spokesmen, Tom Watson of Georgia, received the Populist nomination for the vice presidency. When the nominating speeches were made Friday night, Watson was not the candidate of the extreme midroaders; they preferred Frank Burkitt of Mississippi. But Watson's name had been mentioned among the delegates and in the newspapers in connection with the compromise plan that Marion Butler had advocated. Colorado, Kansas, and other western states stood by Sewall. When the first ballot showed that Watson had a large lead, but not a majority, with Sewall running second, Texas changed from Burkitt to Watson; Tennessee switched from her favorite son, A. L. Mimms, to Watson; as North Carolina prepared to change her vote from Harry Skinner to Watson, the chair announced that the Georgian had won the nomination.[24]

[23] Raleigh *Caucasian*, July 30, 1896. See also the comment in the St. Louis *Globe-Democrat*, July 24, 1896, that the "middle-of-the-road men have acted more like a disorganized mob than anything else since they've been in St. Louis."

[24] Raleigh *Caucasian*, July 30, 1896; New York *Herald*, July 25, 1896; Hicks, *Populist Revolt*, 365; and Bryan, *First Battle*, 270-71. Mann Page of Virginia was also nominated. The New Yorker who placed Sewall's name in nomination did not have a happy task: "Mr. Chairman, in order to draw the poison quickly, and have it out, let me . . . give some reason or try to give some reason why we should nominate" Sewall. (Applause and hisses.) He concluded: "The Vice President does not amount to much unless the President is a consumptive, and 'Billy' Bryan is no consumptive." New York *Times*, July 25, 1896.

Just why Tom Watson, with his long record of strong opposition to fusion of any kind, had consented to play a vital role in a plan designed to bring about quasi-fusion of the Populists and Democrats is a puzzle that may never be solved. Perhaps the best answer is the one that he himself gave shortly after the convention. "I will accept the nomination," he explained, "in the interest of harmony and to prevent disruption of the Populist party, which seemed imminent." Watson added that under the circumstances he fully endorsed the convention's action; furthermore, when he and Bryan had been in the House of Representatives they had "voted together on every measure." Watson subsequently explained that he had been sincere in saying earlier that he would not accept either place on the straight Populist ticket that he had advocated. He added: "I stayed away from the Convention partly to avoid prominence, and the Georgia delegation had positive instructions not to allow the use of my name. . . . When I said I would not accept I did not dream that such a crisis could possibly come upon our party."[25]

In thinking that his candidacy was necessary to "harmonize the factions and save the party" Watson was partly correct. He was hardly the only southern Populist who could have served the purpose, but he was well qualified, aside from an erratic streak that was destined to cause much difficulty in the campaign. Where the real trouble came was in the later assertion by Watson and some of his followers that unnamed Democratic "lobbyists" and Senator Jones had promised that if the Populists would nominate Bryan the Democrats would manage to get Sewall off their ticket.[26]

[25] Atlanta *Constitution*, July 26, 1896; telegram from Watson to New York *Herald*, July 28, 1896.

[26] Alex M. Arnett, *The Populist Movement in Georgia* (New York, 1922), 199, names two of the Georgia delegates who made this claim in 1896 and then told it to him years later. Arnett adds: "Mr. Watson declared to the writer in a recent interview that Jones never denied making such a promise. Jones seems to have ignored the charge." Both Watson and Arnett were

If any of the Georgia delegates in St. Louis telegraphed to Watson that Jones had promised Sewall's withdrawal, and memories rather than documents are the only sources for the story, they were apparently guilty of either unintelligent wishful thinking or distortion of the truth. As early as July 21 accounts had been published of Jones' refusal to discuss any such bargain with Marion Butler; and after a majority of the delegates had voted for Allen for the permanent chairmanship, it was obvious that a solid majority of the Populists at St. Louis intended to nominate Bryan for the presidency. After that vote on July 23, as before it, Jones and the leaders of the extreme fusionists among the Populists worked not to conciliate the extreme midroaders but to secure the Populist nomination of Sewall as well as of Bryan. Not until Butler and the moderate midroaders joined the Texas-led extremists in proceeding first with the nomination of the vice-presidential candidate did the extreme fusionists see their hopes of nominating Sewall too begin to slip away. With a Populist majority established for Bryan, why should any of the Democratic leaders at St. Louis talk about replacing Sewall with a southern Populist?

Aside from these developments at St. Louis, the Democrats were confident after the triumph of the reformers at Chicago

---

wrong. Newspapers before, during, and after the Populist convention carried Jones's emphatic denial of precisely this charge. One example: "I have never stated to any one that there is any likelihood of Mr. Sewall withdrawing from the ticket." Jones to T. M. Patterson, July 24, 1896, in St. Louis *Globe-Democrat*, July 26, 1896. William W. Brewton, *The Life of Thomas E. Watson* (Atlanta, 1926), 268-69, tells virtually the same thing as Arnett. Brewton, an ardent admirer of Watson who had access to his papers after his death, adds that Watson was really not surprised that Sewall would not resign and that "it was only" to prevent the split in the party that he had "wired his consent to fusion." Hicks, *Populist Revolt*, 365, states that "most of the compromisers at St. Louis" believed that the Democrats would withdraw Sewall and cites Arnett and Brewton. Woodward, *Watson*, 298, writes that Watson "was given to understand" that the Democrats would withdraw Sewall and cites an interview with one J. L. Cartledge of Augusta, Georgia, "who wired Watson from St. Louis."

that the Bryan-Sewall ticket would win in the South. Thus Bryan's running mate had been chosen not from the "safe" section but from New England, which was "safe" for the Republicans. In all of the southern midroaders' fulminations against Sewall there ran a deep, sectional resentment that the South had again been bypassed in the selection of candidates for the highest national offices. Southern Populists, for all their brave, and to a large degree successful, efforts to transcend the old sectionalism, were still Southerners who carried their own share of what Professor C. Vann Woodward has called "the burden of Southern history."

That Senator Jones or any other responsible Democrat at St. Louis agreed to try to eliminate Sewall from the race is altogether improbable. What is much more likely is that Marion Butler at St. Louis said, and correctly, that he had done, was doing, and would do everything in his ability to bring about Sewall's withdrawal. Even a political novice might be expected to know that Butler's power concerning a nomination already made by a national Democratic convention was limited. Moreover, his primary purpose was not to eliminate Sewall, as desirable as that might be from his viewpoint and that of other Populists, but to save the national organization of the People's party. This was the purpose which had finally inspired so many outstanding Populists from all sections of the country to cooperate with Butler in the unprecedented program of action undertaken at St. Louis.

The early morning nomination of Watson brought the Populists to the last, and in many ways most delicate, phase of their convention, the nomination of the presidential candidate. It was delicate because the extreme fusionists had argued all along that the nomination of Bryan without Sewall was impossible and that Bryan would not, indeed could not, accept any such nomination. Could the Populists nominate him even if he asked that they not do so?

Many delegates were impatient for the answer to that question as the celebration following Watson's nomination began to die down in the hall. Some had come to the evening session with their luggage in tow. But the time was about 1 A.M. (Saturday, July 25), the end of a long day's exciting developments. Weaver's motion for adjournment was declared by the chair to be carried amid confusion and shouts of "no."[27]

The telegraph, even before the newspapers, kept Bryan in Lincoln fully informed of developments in the Populist convention. Jones had advised him, however, to ignore all embarrassing questions and let his well known record speak for itself.[28] But when the Populists voted to nominate their vice-presidential candidate first, and Sewall's chances faded accordingly, the Democratic national chairman telegraphed Bryan the news, asked him what should be done if Sewall were not nominated by the Populists, and advised him that in such event he (Jones) favored declining a nomination by the Populists.

Bryan responded, before or about the time that the Populists were making their speeches naming the various vice-presidential nominees, that he agreed with Jones and wished his name withdrawn from consideration if Sewall were not nominated also. These telegrams were in the hands of Thomas Patterson of Colorado that evening. The St. Louis newspapers as well as every other daily paper of any size in

---

[27] New York *Herald*, July 25, 1896. Despite the late hour, the argument might be made that Weaver, Allen, and others were afraid to proceed to the nomination of the presidential candidate when Populist partisanship ran high in the wake of Watson's nomination. On the other hand, Bryan's position was still ambiguous as far as most delegates knew at 1 A.M. It would be much less so, and more embarrassing for his Populist supporters, after the morning newspapers appeared.

[28] Jones to Bryan, telegram, July 21, 1896, Bryan MSS. An example of what Jones meant: the Georgia delegation wired Bryan on July 24 asking if he would accept the Populist nomination on the Populist platform, and the penciled notation on the telegram in the Bryan MSS is "not answered."

the nation carried either the texts or the substance of the telegrams on Saturday, July 25, 1896.[29]

In other words, every Populist who attended the last crucial session of the convention on that Saturday had read in the morning newspapers or had otherwise heard that Bryan did not wish to be nominated by the Populists unless Sewall was also. Yet the overwhelming majority of the Populists went ahead and nominated the Nebraskan as their own candidate for the presidency of the United States.

They were not tricked into this action. They did it because they had to do it for the survival of the national People's party and for an excellent fighting chance to win the reforms they and many others desired. The Populist leaders were gambling, for they did not know what Bryan would do; but, being politicians, they knew that candidates never go out of their way to reject votes. In his speech nominating Bryan, General Weaver first established clearly that he too had been won over to the program of Butler and the other moderate midroaders. Then Weaver went straight to the embarrassing news from Nebraska: "You have all read the papers this morning; you have all read the manly dispatch from . . . Bryan. No man could have done less and be a man. . . . But . . . this question has reached a point where neither Mr. Bryan nor his personal friends have any right whatever to say what the action of this convention shall be. This is a greater question than the personality of its candidates."[30]

[29] St. Louis *Globe-Democrat*, St. Louis *Republic*, New York *Herald*, Augusta, Georgia, *Chronicle* (cited by Arnett, *Populist Movement in Georgia*, 200), and Atlanta *Constitution*, all July 25, 1896.

[30] Text of Weaver's speech is in Bryan, *First Battle*, 276-79. Hicks, *Populist Revolt*, 366, Woodward, *Watson*, 300, and other accounts mention Chairman Allen's refusal to read to the convention another telegram from Bryan or to allow Democratic Governor Stone of Missouri to read it during the roll call of the states for nominations. Although this episode has been made a part of the "conspiracy" interpretation, Allen argued that a Democratic governor had no right to the floor of the Populist convention and that he, Allen, was not going to tell the delegates again what they already knew.

General Field of Virginia, the vice-presidential candidate of the Populists' "blue-gray" team of 1892, seconded Bryan's nomination and moved that it be made unanimous. Although Allen was at first inclined to rule the motion in order, angry cries from the extreme midroaders led to a hasty huddle of the leaders on the platform and the decision to proceed with the roll call of states. Six more hours of oratory and nominations followed.

The extremists rallied behind S. F. Norton of Illinois, editor of a Populist newspaper and author of one of the numerous books dealing with the money question. The balloting resulted in 1,042 votes for Bryan, 340 for Norton. After the traditional parade of the state banners and noisy celebration, which Josephus Daniels found about as enthusiastic as the scene he had witnessed when the Democrats named Bryan at Chicago, the exhausted Populists prepared to leave St. Louis.[31]

Henry D. Lloyd commented, soon after the convention, that if the "radicals" at St. Louis had only tried they might have carried the day against the "stultification" represented by Bryan and silver and carried it for "a 'stalwart' ticket" on a platform demanding "public ownership of all monopolies." Such an interpretation was obviously quite misleading about the temper and the composition of the convention. Lloyd, moreover, had a telegram in his pocket from Debs saying, "Please do not permit the use of my name for nomination."

It should be noted also that in none of his various telegrams did Bryan say categorically that he would not accept a Populist nomination, if it were proffered, even in the face of his published request that he not be nominated without Sewall. Ignatius Donnelly raised this question without getting an answer in the convention's last session. See Martin Ridge, *Ignatius Donnelly: The Portrait of a Politician* (Chicago, 1962), 356.

[31] New York *Herald*, July 26, 1896; Raleigh *Caucasian*, July 30, 1896. Some accounts give fewer votes for Norton, but 340 seems to be correct. Eleven or twelve votes were scattered among Ignatius Donnelly, Eugene Debs, and Jacob S. Coxey.

And Clarence Darrow, among others, advised Lloyd not to make the "radical" speech that he had all ready for delivery to convention.[32]

Such a struggle as the Populists had waged at St. Louis left serious divisions in the party. Yet the important fact was that the great majority of the party and its leaders had held together thus far for Bryan and national reforms. The campaign ahead posed difficult problems for the Populists as well as for Bryan. Tom Watson, as subsequent events would reveal, had allowed himself to be sadly miscast in the political drama. But under the leadership of Marion Butler, whom the Populist national committee elected as national chairman of the party at the conclusion of the convention, the bulk of the Populists prepared to fight valiantly for Bryan and free silver.

[32] Lloyd, "The Populists at St. Louis," 303; Caro Lloyd, *Henry D. Lloyd,* I, 262. Norman Pollack, *The Populist Response to Industrial America: Midwestern Populist Thought* (Cambridge, Mass., 1962), 103-105, is an intellectual history which persuasively argues that fusion meant "the last chance to advance radicalism" and was "a long-term groping toward effective radical action."

The Campaign: First Phase

A s THE Populist delegates returned to their homes from the St. Louis convention, there was much confusion as to whether a genuine union of the silver forces had or had not been made possible. True, the Populists had nominated William Jennings Bryan, the Democratic standard bearer, as their own candidate for the presidency. But they had also rebelled, in order to prevent the threatened bolt of a large faction from the South and to preserve the independent organization of the party, and had named Tom Watson of Georgia as their own vice-presidential candidate to run with Bryan.

Under the presidential electoral system the voter casts his ballot for a slate of electors in each state, rather than directly for the candidates. Everyone saw, therefore, that if a slate of Bryan-Sewall (Democratic) electors competed in each state where the Populists were strong with a slate of Bryan-Watson (Populist) electors, the effect would be the same as if the Populists had not nominated Bryan. The reform vote would be split and the Republican chances for victory vastly enhanced.

The solution of cooperative or fusion electoral tickets that was eventually worked out in most states may appear, from the perspective of hindsight, foreordained. But to contemporaries such was certainly not the case, and a welter of conflicting ideas and schemes developed before the main outlines of a workable plan of union could emerge. Even then there were Populists, and conspicuously Tom Watson, who never accepted the cooperative plan that the large majority of the leaders of both parties came to support.[1]

Sewall, the target of bitter attacks from southern Populists, played a quiet but on the whole a generous role in the tangled situation. Upon learning of his rejection by the Populists, Sewall immediately declared to Bryan: "I desire that you will do just what you believe is best for the success of the head of our ticket. The principles we are fighting for are so paramount to any personal relations that the latter should not have any weight or influence whatever with your action. I cannot for a moment allow myself to be a factor in any action on your part that would, in the slightest degree, hazard an electoral vote for you."[2]

Sewall's personal generosity notwithstanding, Bryan faced a difficult situation. He had explicitly requested that the Populists not nominate him without also naming his running mate from Maine. Now if he repudiated the Populist nomination he stood to lose hundreds of thousands of votes and make union of the nation's reform groups impossible. If, on the other hand, he accepted the Populist nomination how could he do so without appearing to ignore the interests of Sewall? And if he accepted the Populist platform along with the

---

[1] Samuel W. Williams, a Populist of Vincennes, Indiana, claimed to have originated at St. Louis the idea of nominating the vice-presidential candidate first. Soon after the convention Williams proposed joint electoral tickets in each state; the Democrats would name half of the electors and the Populists half. Each party would still run its own ticket, though the electors would be the same on each. Then in each state where the Democratic-Populist electors won the election the state's total vote would be given, before the meeting of the electoral college, to the vice-presidential candidate of the party whose ticket had received the most votes in the state. New York *Times,* August 2, 1896. Nothing ever came of this plan at the time, probably because at first each side hoped the other's vice-presidential candidate would get out of the race. But ultimately a plan partly resembling Williams' scheme was adopted, as will be explained below.

[2] Sewall to Bryan, July 25, 1896, Bryan MSS; also Bryan, *First Battle,* 298.

nomination he would surely add strength to the bolt of the Gold Democrats, who charged that Bryan was not a true Democrat but a Populist anyhow.

The Nebraskan handled the thorny issue gingerly but candidly. In a statement to the reporters crowded into Lincoln, Bryan first reviewed the telegrams that he and Senator Jones had exchanged during the last two days of the Populist convention. "I appreciate the desire, manifested at St. Louis, to consolidate all the free silver forces," Bryan declared, "and regret that they did not nominate Mr. Sewall also. He stands squarely upon the Chicago platform and has defended our cause against greater opposition than we have had to meet in the West and South." Admitting that the Populist platform was "substantially identical" to the Democratic one on many issues, Bryan pointed out that the Populists also endorsed some policies of which he did not approve. "All that I can now say is that my action will depend entirely upon the conditions attached to the nomination," he concluded. "I shall do nothing which will endanger the success of bimetallism, nor shall I do anything unfair to Mr. Sewall."[3]

Marion Butler, elated over the success of the strategy that he had sponsored at the Populist convention, declared that only one thing stood in the way of "certain victory" for reform since the Populists had met the Democrats more than half way: "Now, if Mr. Sewall will be patriotic and withdraw from the Democratic ticket as a candidate for Vice-President he will remove the only obstacle to a complete unification of all the voters who oppose the single gold standard and victory will be assured from the hour that he takes that high and patriotic position."[4] In reply to a similar suggestion from a reporter, Sewall fired back: "Resign? I never withdraw and

[3] New York *Herald*, July 26, 1896; Bryan, *First Battle*, 297.
[4] Raleigh *News and Observer*, July 26, 1896.

I never resign. I was nominated by the Democratic Convention and I am a Democrat."[5]

In view of the uncertainty about Bryan's acceptance of the nomination, one of the last actions of the Populist convention had been to grant plenary power, that is, power equivalent to that of the party convention itself, to the party's national committee. That committee met shortly after the adjournment of the convention and elected Marion Butler as the party's national chairman. Although Butler, at this initial stage of the campaign, clearly shared Tom Watson's hope of eliminating Sewall, newspaper rumors telling a different story added to the confusion. The New York *Herald* and St. Louis *Globe-Democrat*, for example, carried far-fetched stories to the effect that the Populist national committee, after conferring with Jones and other Democratic leaders, had decided to ask Watson to retire from the Populist ticket so that the committee could exercise its plenary power to name Sewall as the Populist candidate for the vice presidency.[6]

Aside from the question of one or the other vice-presidential candidate's withdrawing from the contest, it was also uncertain whether Bryan should be officially notified of his nomination by the Populists. Ignatius Donnelly, who had finally swung around to support the Populist nomination of Bryan, had pled to the convention for a generous policy that would not put Bryan in an embarrassing position and force him to choose between Watson and Sewall. "Neither do I think we ought to call upon him to indorse our platform," Donnelly had asserted. "Our principles do not exist by the sufferance of William J. Bryan or any man on earth."[7]

[5] New York *Herald*, July 26, 1896.

[6] July 26, 1896. Other members of the Populist national executive committee were: John W. Breidenthal of Kansas, John S. Dore of California, J. A. Edgerton of Nebraska, M. C. Rankin of Indiana, H. W. Reed of Georgia, James R. Sovereign of Arkansas, Dr. C. F. Taylor of Pennsylvania, and George F. Washburn of Massachusetts.

[7] Atlanta *Constitution*, July 26, 1896.

But there were those Populists, mostly midroaders from the South, who felt more animosity than generosity toward Bryan and who were still grasping at straws to thwart the majority's preference. After the adjournment of the Populist convention, anti-Bryan Texans took over the auditorium and invited other midroaders to join them in a caucus. This group of dissidents named Henry D. Lloyd and two others as a committee to ascertain if Bryan in his various telegrams to St. Louis had said that he would refuse to accept the Populist nomination. Another committee headed by one Henry L. Call of New York was empowered to name a full Populist ticket headed by Tom Watson in case Bryan had not accepted the Populist nomination within thirty days. Although these threats of bolting came from small minorities representing opposite extremes of the party, their mood is well illustrated by the statement allegedly made by Milton Park, Texan midroader and editor of the *Southern Mercury*: "If Bryan's name is not taken off the ticket we will go back to Texas and raise Old Ned. We will give the Republicans the electoral ticket, and we will take the State ticket for our share of the fruit."[8]

In the face of such recrimination and confusion, some of Bryan's advisers urged him to cut the Gordian knot by rejecting the Populist nomination. The Democratic governor of Missouri, William J. Stone, did not believe that either of the vice-presidential candidates could be withdrawn. Difficulties surrounded the matter of cooperative electoral tickets. Therefore, Stone argued, Bryan should encircle himself with his prominent Populist supporters such as General Weaver and Senator Allen and with Silver Republican leaders and tactfully decline to run on the ticket with Watson rather than imperil the reform cause by running with the two vice-presidential candidates.[9] The Democratic national chairman,

[8] New York *Herald*, July 26, 28; New York *Times*, July 26, 27, 1896.
[9] Stone to Senator Jones, July 31, 1896, Bryan MSS.

fresh from a conference with Bryan, shunned the drastic course recommended by Governor Stone and telegraphed the Atlanta *Constitution* that while he could not consider any scheme for the withdrawal of Sewall he would promote as best he could "any just and fair proposition for fusion on electoral ticket."[10]

If Jones had next embarked on a studied policy of silence while the smoke settled, Bryan's cause would have benefitted. But Tom Watson kept the wires warm with his own challenging statements to the newspapers, and Jones unwisely retaliated. In addition to exclusive statements telegraphed to the New York *Herald* and New York *World*, both of which anti-Bryan papers delighted in stirring up as much trouble as possible for the silverites, Watson threatened through his own weekly organ, the *People's Party Paper*, that if Sewall declined to withdraw for harmony's sake "the rank and file of our party may break away from the leaders and refuse to vote for Mr. Bryan at all."[11]

Provoked by these threats, Senator Jones gave an interview, which he subsequently tried to disavow, depicting the Southern delegates to the Populist convention as generally "not a creditable class" who had practically admitted that "they were out for nothing but spoil." He expected these men to "do all they can to harass the Democracy and create confusion, and in the end they will do just as they are doing now in Alabama, fuse with the Republicans and vote for McKinley. They will go with the negroes, where they belong." Watson might think that he could bluff the Democrats but, Jones insisted, "Mr. Sewall will, of course, remain on the ticket, and Mr. Watson can do what he likes."[12]

[10] July 31, 1896.
[11] Atlanta *Constitution*, July 30, 1896.
[12] New York *World*, August 3, 1896, as quoted in the Raleigh *Caucasian*, August 6, 1896; also Woodward, *Watson*, 310. For Jones' prompt denial of part of this story see St. Louis *Post-Dispatch*, August 4, 1896.

Marion Butler attempted to halt the fast developing feud between Watson and Jones. The Populist chairman announced that he refused to believe that the Democratic chairman had been quoted correctly. "What a humiliating and sickening spectacle it would be," Butler remonstrated, "should the folly of personal ambition and demon of party spirit step into, confuse and divide the allied majority and deliver the people into the hands of the enemies of republican institutions." He thought that it would be "better for candidates and chairmen to do less talking at the present," for "in spite of the indiscretions of individuals and so-called leaders, the American people have determined to win the fight and they will do it."[13]

Despite the difficulties and irritations inevitably connected with cooperation between the Democrats and Populists, Chairman Butler's optimism was not without a solid base. The campaign had not really begun yet, and headquarters had not been selected, much less opened. But contemporaries as well as historians concur in the generalization that a groundswell of enthusiasm for Bryan and silver swept over large segments of the population during the late summer. It would be October before Chairman Mark Hanna's superb organization and unprecedentedly vast treasury would begin to bring cheering signs to the Republicans. Meantime, attention during August focused on the Populist and Democratic state conventions where, often regardless of what national party chairmen might prefer, the state party units worked out their own versions of cooperation or, in some cases, noncooperation.

Before the end of the campaign Democrats and Populists in twenty-eight states, including all of the crucial states of the upper Midwest where the decisive battle occurred, reached some type of cooperative agreement on the electoral ticket. But that total of twenty-eight states was not reached without

[13] Raleigh *News and Observer*, August 6, 1896.

much complicated maneuvering and negotiating, and there were states where fusion failed significantly.

In Georgia a tense convention of some 5,000 Populists responded to Tom Watson's oratory with wild enthusiasm. Emphasizing the sectional theme on which he would continue to capitalize, Watson attacked Sewall and cried: "My God, hasn't the South played second fiddle long enough? Your 156 votes insure the election of any man who can carry any decent support outside of the South. I appeal to Southern pride and to Southern manhood to seize the opportunity to link with the West and throw off the domination of the North and East."[14] Despite his declaration that he would try to get every vote for Bryan whether he, Watson, went down to defeat or not, his strategy aimed at getting Sewall off and Watson onto the Democratic national ticket. After injecting a new issue into the state campaign by nominating a Prohibitionist for governor, the Georgia Populists, with Watson's smiling approval, empowered their state executive committee to withdraw a fair proportion of the thirteen Populist electors for Bryan and Watson and substitute Democratic electors but to do this only after Sewall's withdrawal from the race. In other words, the Georgia Populists had acted boldly in accordance with the slogan that some midroaders applauded, "No Watson, no Bryan."[15]

In Kansas, the stronghold of western Populism, the matter of Bryan's two running mates was viewed quite differently. When the Kansas Democrats indicated their willingness to let the Populists name the full state ticket in exchange for the Democrat's naming all ten of the Kansas electors, the

[14] Atlanta *Constitution*, August 7, and New York *Herald*, August 8, 1896.
[15] Atlanta *Constitution*, August 8, 1896. There was much truth in the *Constitution's* argument that the Populists had named their own vice-presidential candidate not because they objected to Sewall but in order to preserve their party organization; and since Watson's nomination was a Populist party measure, it should be so accepted without any discrediting of Sewall. Thus the Atlanta newspaper favored electoral fusion. *Ibid.*, August 1, 1896.

Populists agreed. In other words, while the Georgia Populists maneuvered to give Watson all of Georgia's electoral votes, the Kansas Populists agreed, in effect, that Sewall should have all of Kansas' votes.[16]

Neither the Georgia nor the Kansas Populists typified the slowly emerging pattern of national cooperation among the reform parties in 1896. North Carolina, as much as any important Populist state, would eventually do that. But Marion Butler, because he initially hoped to inspire Sewall's withdrawal and to do so without Watson's angry and open intransigence, was slow to reveal his hand.

In North Carolina, cooperation between Populists and Republicans in 1894 had led to the first defeat of the Democrats since Reconstruction, and the "Fusionist" legislature had enacted fairer election laws, restored home rule to the counties, and elected Marion Butler and a Republican, Jeter Pritchard, to the United States Senate. There was great pressure from many Populists in 1896 for a continuation of this cooperation in state elections, but the reformers' capture of the national Democratic party and the sharpening of national political issues complicated the matter.

Fusion between Tarheel Populists and Republicans was never fully developed because Butler and a majority of his party refused to support Republican candidates for federal office, especially Pritchard for a full term in the Senate, unless they gave impressive proof of their support for free silver. North Carolina Republicans, like those in the West, did not openly embrace the monometallic gold standard, as did eastern Republicans and the Cleveland Democrats. Rather, farmstate Republicans emphasized the call for "international bimetallism" in the Republican platform and insisted that the surest, safest way to restore silver was to elect McKinley.[17]

[16] Raleigh *News and Observer*, August 6; New York *Herald*, August 8, 1896.
[17] Atlanta *Constitution*, August 1, 1896; Raleigh *News and Observer*, August 16, 1896.

Despite the late and dubious conversion of these Republicans to the cause of financial reform, Butler led a large majority of his North Carolina Populist followers in drawing a strict line between state and national affairs and doing nothing that would imperil or be inconsistent with national reforms. Still, because of his continuing hope to have Watson become Bryan's only running mate, he refused to rush into the electoral fusion which the Democrats proffered in North Carolina.

Resigning his post as state Populist chairman, Butler proceeded to Washington where the Populist national executive committee held its first meeting of the campaign on August 18. Important decisions desperately needed making, for Populists throughout the nation were confused as to what their policy should be. Were they to put out separate Bryan-Watson electoral tickets or not? Were they to say, as many Texan midroaders did, that if Sewall did not withdraw they did not care if McKinley won and might even vote for him?[18]

Watson, for some reason still avoiding crucial meetings of national Populist leaders, had "other engagements" that kept him from sitting with the executive committee. But the member of the committee from Georgia, H. W. Reed, had Watson's "entire confidence" and would serve as his personal representative. Watson reported that many Democrats in the South were demanding Sewall's retirement, and he felt sure that if the Populist committee took and held a "bold position" Jones and his colleagues would surrender.[19]

[18] The Butler MSS for August 1896 are filled with inquiries, pleas, and threats from Populists across the country.

[19] Watson to Butler, August 8, 1896, Butler MSS. Watson and other Populists continually attacked Sewall as a "plutocrat" because of his connection at one time with a national bank and with a railway corporation. Ironically, Reed, who served as Watson's representative and traveling companion throughout the campaign, was a prominent businessman in Brunswick, Georgia, who resigned the presidency of the national bank there for the reason that his "connection with the national executive committee of the people's party would unquestionably complicate the bank's relations"

Meeting, then, without Tom Watson, the Populist leaders, like their Democratic counterparts, decided that having campaign headquarters only in Washington would not be strategic for the massive effort that was beginning in the upper midwest. The Democrats opened their main headquarters in Chicago, even though no important daily newspaper there supported Bryan. The Populists decided on a branch headquarters in Chicago to be run by George F. Washburn, a native of Massachusetts and veteran Populist, and by John R. Sovereign, head of the Knights of Labor and also a Populist executive committeeman. Butler, who would remain in the Washington offices, told waiting reporters what the Populists leaders had decided in their meeting: "The People's party ticket as named at St. Louis is Bryan and Watson, and that will be the People's party ticket until the polls close in November. Mr. Bryan is as much our candidate as Mr. Watson, and as far as this committee has the power it will strive just as hard to elect one as the other, and will leave nothing in its power undone to help either or both, but it will not help one candidate at the expense of the other."[20]

As soon as Reed had informed him of the executive committee's decisions, Watson assured Butler that he was "in hearty accord with the conclusions reached." Watson appreciated the "bold position the Committee has taken in reference to the St. Louis ticket" and asserted his desire "to act in thorough harmony with the Committee."[21] But the Georgian apparently had misunderstood the true thrust of the committee's policy and of Butler's statement.

The key phrase in the published statement was the last one in which the chairman declared that the Populist national

---

and because he had to devote his time to the campaign. Earlier, Reed had been associated with the Savannah, Florida and Western Railway. *Atlanta Constitution*, August 27, 1896.

[20] St. Louis *Post-Dispatch*, August 19, 1896.

[21] Watson to Butler, August 21, 1896, Butler MSS.

leaders would "not help one candidate at the expense of the other." This phrase really meant that the committee would not necessarily support separate Bryan-Watson electoral tickets, which policy Watson insisted upon as long as Sewall remained on the Democratic ticket, because the separate tickets would hurt Bryan's chances by splitting the reform vote. Nor, on the other hand, did Butler and his colleagues countenance the Kansas Populists' action which had, in effect, sacrificed Watson. In other words, Butler's hope of getting Sewall out of the race by an ambiguous policy concerning the presidential electoral tickets was coming to a swift end. Pressure from Bryan's Populist supporters and confusion among all Populists required that ambiguity cease. Populist national policy became clearer, therefore, and as the overwhelming majority of the national Populist leaders called and worked for fusion with the Democrats on the various states' electoral tickets, Tom Watson's frustration and fury increased. And Marion Butler, more than anyone else, became the target for the wrath of the unhappy candidate.

Butler's initial statement for the committee was followed by others which clarified several key matters. A reporter asked what the Populist national executive committee thought about a state (such as Kansas) in which Democrats and Populists fused, with the Populists taking the state ticket and the Democrats all of the electors. Butler replied with what he described as the unanimous opinion of the executive committee: "We have no official information that this has been done in any State. If it has been done or is contemplated, the National committee will not approve or recognize it. The highest law in any party is the action of its National convention. No man or State or organization can be disloyal to such supreme authority of a party without arraying themselves in direct and hostile opposition to the National convention." Butler added that the committee would not insist on straight Bryan-Watson tickets in every state but that "wherever Populists and Democrats join forces on the electoral ticket there must be a due and proper recognition of each party's candidates by a just and equitable division of electors."[22]

Although he still had his own private hopes of eliminating Sewall, officially and publicly the Populist national chairman had retreated along the lines dictated by the wishes of the Populist executive committee as well as by the inexorable logic of the situation. But Butler blundered when he announced that there would be no formal notification of nomination to Bryan and Watson. He first said that this was because the Populist candidates in 1892 had not been formally notified and because it was the "mission of the Populists to depart from many of the useless practices and customs followed by the old parties."[23]

Butler's statement implied that there would be no notification at all. But what he probably meant to say, and what the committee apparently had decided, was that there would be no ceremony or meeting at the time of notification, as was traditional with the older parties. Rather, the Populists would merely notify by letter and at a time still to be announced. Butler's initial statement, however, did suggest that the Populists would not notify Bryan and Watson.

Watson promptly fired back a correction: Generals Weaver and Field had been notified by letters in 1892. Furthermore, the Populist party would now occupy a humiliating position if it "virtually says it fears to notify Mr. Bryan, lest he should

[22] Raleigh *News and Observer*, August 21, 1896. Privately Butler took an even stronger stand in defense of the Populist party's rights: "The People's party is entitled to more electors than its proportional part of the vote will justify on the ground that we have already put at the head of our ticket a man nominated by the Democrats." Butler to J. H. Hobson of Virginia, August 29, 1896, Butler MSS.

[23] New York *Herald*, August 24, 1896.

repudiate the nomination." Watson added that he himself would be sorely humiliated to be forced into a canvass without having been notified.

More importantly, Watson now understood the true drift of the Populist executive committee's decisions, and he did not at all approve. He concentrated on driving Sewall out of the race and believed that the only way to do that was for all Populists to support only Bryan-Watson tickets. "Every one of these 'fusions,' whereby electors are divided between Sewall and Watson," he declared, "stultifies the Populist who votes the fusion ticket." Despite all his talk about objecting to fusion on principle, Watson actually objected to Sewall rather than fusion, as this statement made clear: "As the nominee of our party, I respectfully ask that we repudiate the fusion policy—unless Sewall is withdrawn."

Watson explained that in deference to the committee's views he had ceased to edit his *People's Party Paper*. And as for the exclusive articles which he had been giving to New York newspapers ever since his nomination at St. Louis, Watson stated that he would write no more—without giving the committee due notice. "I recognize your right to guide the management of the campaign, & will co-operate cordially & earnestly," Watson insisted to Butler, "but upon questions involving principle I must claim the right to my own opinions."[24] Watson and the national leadership of the Populist party, as well as the majority of the party's membership outside the deep South apparently, were about to come to an embarrassing split over the "principle" of Sewall's continued candidacy for the vice presidency.

Actually, the committee meant all along to notify Bryan and Watson but to delay doing so until after the Democrats and Silver Republicans had notified Bryan on September 8.

[24] Watson to Butler, August 24, 1896, Butler MSS.

The Populist leaders also regarded mid-September as an auspicious time because this would be immediately after the early state election in Maine, where the only question in anyone's mind was just how large a margin of victory the Republicans would have. In the face of the expected crushing defeat of the Democrats in Sewall's own state, surely the Democratic leaders would be ready to talk about sacrificing the hapless Sewall. Pressure from Watson and his midroad sympathizers, however, forced the Populist leaders to clarify and announce their plans.

Despite his qualified pledge to cease his personal campaign in the newspapers, Watson signed an editorial in his *People's Party Paper* which ripped into the committee and Butler on the matter of notification. Anti-Bryan newspapers in New York and throughout the nation reveled in the public disharmony in the silver camp, and not only played up Watson's attack on the Populist leadership but shed crocodile tears over the allegedly shabby treatment being given the Georgian.[25] "You must realize as fully as I do," Butler rebuked Watson, "that our party is not being benefitted by such exhibitions through the press, whether they are correct or not." To Reed, who sympathized with Watson but desired to "keep a padlock on his centrifugal tendency," Butler remonstrated that the executive committee, as Reed well knew from his participation in the meeting, had had no purpose "to do anything prejudicial" to Watson. "It is impossible to run a successful campaign," Butler groaned, "if there is to be constant friction advertised in the newspapers between our candidates and our committee."[26]

[25] New York *Herald*, August 27, 1896; the New York *Tribune's* applause for Watson's "courageous and persistent efforts to compel a serious recognition of his candidacy at the hands of the Altgeld-Tillman-Bryan managers and their Populist allies" is quoted in Woodward, *Watson*, 317.

[26] Butler to Watson, Butler to Reed, August 27, 1896, Campaign Letterbooks, Butler MSS; Reed to Butler, August 30, 1896, Butler MSS.

Hasty conferences among the Populist and Democratic leaders in Washington led to the decision that the Populists should announce their plans to notify their candidates officially. Bryan had sent his approval of the move, apparently on the condition that nothing embarrassing about the vice-presidential matter be included in the formal letter of notification. Bryan did not need to worry on this score since he would be notified by one of his staunchest Populist supporters, Senator William V. Allen, who had served as permanent chairman of the St. Louis convention. Butler, who had been the temporary chairman, would notify the Populists' unhappy vice-presidential candidate.[27]

In response to Reed's urgent request for a conference before he and Watson left for campaign appointments in Dallas and other western cities, Butler agreed to meet them in Atlanta. Watson, whose distrust of Butler had quickly taken deep root, coolly declared: "As to meeting me in Atlanta, or elsewhere, you can exercise your pleasure. Thus far you have treated me with no consideration, and a continuance of that spirit of disrespect will neither surprise nor offend me."[28]

[27] New York *Herald*, August 29, 1896; Butler to L. C. Bateman, August 29, 1896, Campaign Letterbooks, Butler MSS. Bateman, a midroader of Maine and Populist candidate for governor, wrote Populists around the country in an effort to enlist support for a notification designed to put Bryan on the spot. Although Bateman styled himself secretary of the notification committee, he represented only the caucus of midroaders that had met after the adjournment of the St. Louis convention. He had written Butler soon after that convention that if Butler and Senator Jones did not persuade the Bryan Democrats of Maine to endorse him in his campaign for governor, there could be no cooperation between Populists and Democrats on the electoral ticket. Bateman failed to gain the Maine Democrats' help and became widely publicized during the presidential campaign as a leader (who had an infinitesimal local following) of the "No Watson, no Bryan" group. Bateman to Butler, July 29, 1896; C. E. Sugg of Henderson, Kentucky, was one of several who informed Butler about Bateman's efforts to manage the notification; Sugg added that he was not one to work for McKinley's election "to spite those with whom I have had conflict." Sugg to Butler, August 22, 1896, Butler MSS.
[28] Watson to Butler, September 1, 1896, Butler MSS.

Butler had, in truth, blundered about the notification. But he had promptly retrieved the error, and Watson did him an injustice in blaming him for the inevitable difficulties of the complicated campaign. With the opening of headquarters, Butler was plunged into the political negotiations that were proceeding among the various parties supporting Bryan and silver in all sections of the country except New England, where there were not enough Populists to warrant much attention. Butler's bulky campaign letterbooks reveal that he stood loyally by Tom Watson. He also journeyed to Atlanta for the meeting that Watson seemed to regard with indifference.

The Atlanta *Constitution* carried a large engraving on its front page of the confrontation between Butler and Watson in the lobby of Atlanta's Kimball House. Although their greetings were reportedly cordial and the private conference lasted throughout the day, newspapermen learned little about the discussion. Repeating his argument that the Democrats should support Watson because he and Bryan truly represented the same principles, Butler expressed his belief that the "people of the south will support Watson," who "represents southern interests." Georgia Populists concluded from Butler's brief statement that he shared their (and Watson's) determination to refuse fusion unless Sewall withdrew; but to believe this they had to ignore Butler's additional statement that there would be no attempt on the part of the Populists to embarrass Bryan in the forthcoming notification.[29]

The conference in Atlanta clearly removed none of the conflicts between Watson's and the executive committee's reading of the situation, but there was at least a temporary truce. As Watson proceeded to Texas, Butler returned to Washington to cope with problems that largely had to do

[29] Atlanta *Constitution*, September 4, 5, 1896.

with the arranging of fusion electoral tickets and the Populists' acute lack of financial resources.

At the height of the campaign, Bryan conferred with other Democratic leaders. After the conference he told reporters, "We are down to our normal condition—without money."[30] This condition characterized the Populists even more than the Democrats, and in view of their almost absolute poverty, the Populists performed miracles to make the effort in the campaign that they did. "If we can have but one cent for every ten dollars used by the enemy," Butler proclaimed in a public appeal for contributions, "we could carry on a vigorous campaign that would mean [McKinley's] defeat."[31] At the outset of the campaign, Butler hoped that an appeal directly to the people for contributions of $1.00 would not only result in the collection of a large sum of money but also in "the gratuitous performance of work for our cause" that would be worth even more than the actual money. Since the corporation and business sources from whence campaign funds for both parties had largely come in the past were all supporting McKinley, Butler hoped that the common people would see the necessity of uniting and contributing.[32]

Such hopes proved illusory, simply because the depression that had begun in 1893 still kept the rank-and-file Populists, as well as their potential sympathizers, in abject poverty. The Populists' national headquarters found it impossible to pay expenses of speakers even when they were going into the hard-fought states of Indiana and Illinois. Political literature, which farmers especially still studied carefully, was available from national Populist headquarters but state and county committees had to buy it at cost.

[30] New York *Times*, September 30, 1896.
[31] Raleigh *Caucasian*, September 17, 1896.
[32] Butler to Senator James K. Jones, August 24, 1896, Campaign Letter-books, Butler MSS. The appeal to the public appeared on September 8, 1896; see St. Louis *Post-Dispatch* of that date.

State organizations were little better off than national headquarters. From Iowa, for example, a farm state that the silver forces wanted and needed to win, the secretary of the Populist party sent word that literature was essential if the state was to be carried for Bryan. He complained that the Republicans were receiving literature from their national headquarters by the freight-car load and sending it out over the state by the wagon load. With $7.00 in cash on hand for the Populist fight in Iowa, the secretary confessed to feeling discouraged and begged for any free literature that might be available.[33]

James R. Sovereign, the labor leader and Populist executive committeeman, had gone to Chicago to run a "Bryan-Free Silver Campaign Labor Bureau." He reported that local labor organizations had at least contributed "very limited aid" to his operation, but in Arkansas, his native state, the Populist voters were so poor that candidates for office were assessed before they could get their names on the ticket. Butler replied that the news from Sovereign was the same as came from the other states. "It is not only very disappointing, but it is really very distressing," Butler declared. "Is it possible that our people have gotten so poor that they cannot even keep headquarters open in making a fight against the . . . gigantic combination of the enemy?" Although barely able to keep stamps and stationery in the headquarters office, Butler insisted that the sad state of affairs should be kept from the public; it would give too much satisfaction to the enemy.[34]

One of the myths that Butler had to fight was that western silver magnates were handsomely financing the Bryan crusade. He wrote the president of the Western Federation of Miners in Colorado that he, Butler, could certainly understand why

[33] E. T. Meredith to J. A. Edgerton, September 11, 1896, Butler MSS.
[34] Sovereign to Butler, September 24, 1896, Butler to Sovereign, September 26, 1896, Campaign Letterbooks, Butler MSS.

the miners were outraged by the injustices done them by the mine operators; but the miners could not afford to let those injustices drive them into helping McKinley in order to hurt the operators. Farmers and wage-earners, Butler argued, had lost twice as much by the demonetization of silver as the mineowners had. Furthermore, Populist headquarters had not received "one cent of contribution from the mine owners of the West," so the miners themselves had every reason to stand by their colaborers all over the country.[35]

To the Populist state committees that begged for aid and pointed to the lavish assistance coming to local Republicans from Hanna's immense funds, Butler replied that, "Whenever any National committee is able to raise funds to send to State committees, you may rest assured that that party is mortgaged to those who furnish the money."[36] Such philosophizing, however true and penetrating, was probably scanty consolation, but it was the best that Butler could do.

Small contributions did come in, and the headquarters offices in Washington and Chicago were kept open and functioning throughout the campaign. Butler and his associates maintained the tremendous correspondence that was one of their principal contributions to the fight. And Butler, financially harassed as the Populists were, remained firm in his belief that "the people are so intensely in earnest on this financial question that it will be impossible for the millions of Republican money to seriously debauch the election."[37]

The lack of money did not prevent the Populist leaders from playing key roles in the gradual consolidation of the various silver groups. The negotiations were often complicated and tortuous, but in state after state Populists, Bryan Democrats, and Silver Republicans were brought into coali-

[35] Butler to Edward Boyce, October 5, 1896, *ibid.*
[36] Butler to James A. Daniel, September 15, 1896, *ibid.*
[37] Butler to Wharton Barker, October 2, 1896, *ibid.*

tions that were as harmonious and effective as could be expected under the circumstances. The situation differed from one state to another, and there were endless complications with reference to the state and congressional as well as the electoral tickets. But a few examples may serve to clarify the general outlines of the Populist contribution to the allied effort for Bryan and national reforms.

In North Carolina, which had the strongest Populist party in the southeast, all observers agreed that unless the Populists and Democrats cooperated on the electoral ticket the Republicans would carry the state for McKinley. Despite this situation, Marion Butler, as mentioned earlier, had restrained the Tarheel Populists from accepting the offer made at the end of July of five of the state's eleven electors. Hoping to find some way to inspire Sewall's retirement, Butler had refrained from decisive action in the one state where his own personal influence was greatest—and where action was bound to speak more clearly than all the statements in the world.

There was also the fact that the Democrats in several southern states (such as Virginia and the deep southern states) felt sure of being able to carry their states without Populist help and were accordingly disdainful of cooperation. Moderate Populists like Butler as well as the midroad faction bitterly resented this Democratic attitude and hoped to hold back on cooperation where it was needed in order to secure a more favorable treatment of Populists in other states. But the hope of downing Sewall loomed largest in Butler's strategy of delaying electoral fusion in North Carolina.

The climax of the Populist campaign to inspire Sewall's withdrawal came immediately after the smashing Republican victory in Maine in mid-September. Even Sewall had publicly predicted such an outcome, since, according to him, three months earlier there had not been "5,000 free silver men in Maine."[38] But when the Republicans increased their margin of victory even in Bath, Sewall's home, the Populists seized on what they hoped would be the final and most damning indictment of the Democratic nominee for the vice presidency. "Mr. Sewall should certainly withdraw, and the State of Maine also says so," George F. Washburn announced from the Populists' Chicago headquarters. Washburn thought that the critical phase of the campaign had arrived, and the "only way to unite" the reform forces was for the Democrats to take Watson, whom Butler had notified in a letter that went out simultaneously with Allen's to Bryan.[39]

Butler conferred at length with Jones when the Democratic chairman visited Washington in mid-September. Rumors about the withdrawal of Sewall or Watson or of both men filled the newspapers, but the actual outcome of the conference was to further the plan of cooperation on the electoral ticket. Bryan clearly would hear of nothing else. Sewall had repeatedly denied all the rumors about his withdrawal but had written Jones that, "In all states where fusions seem to you desirable and important for the election of Mr. Bryan, I want my personal consideration to be entirely disregarded to that end."[40] Butler, pressed by reporters and embarrassed by midroaders who had attributed certain anti-Sewall statements to him, met the issue straight on: "I have never, either directly or indirectly, received any assurance that Mr. Sewall would be withdrawn, glad as I should be to receive such assurance, believing that it would make the election of Bryan absolutely certain."[41]

Privately, Butler had finally come to recognize aspects of the matter that helped him reconcile himself to Sewall's

38 St. Louis *Post-Dispatch*, September 15, 1896.
39 New York *Herald*, September 16, 1896.
40 Sewall to Jones, August 31, 1896, Bryan MSS.
41 New York *Herald*, September 16, 1896.

remaining in the race. In several long letters to Washburn, written shortly after Butler had conferred with Bryan, the Populist chairman analyzed the pros and the cons of the vice-presidential situation. Suppose Sewall offered to withdraw if Watson would do the same? What would Watson do? If he refused, would not the Democrats gain moral prestige over the Populists? Or if Watson should agree to withdraw, would not the midroaders cause even more trouble than they already were causing? More importantly, Butler faced the question of how Sewall's withdrawal in favor of Watson would affect Bryan's chances in the pivotal north central states of Indiana, Illinois, Michigan, Minnesota, and Iowa. Although the Populist vote might be crucial there, these were not Populist strongholds nor did they fit easily into the sectional pattern of South and West versus East that Watson emphasized. Butler thought that if the Democrats were to foresee defeat they might be glad to withdraw Sewall "so that they could say they acceded to our demands but that Watson was the load that defeated the ticket." Even though these Democrats might be wrong, Butler felt sure that they would use the argument.

Butler clinched his argument for sitting tight and accepting the accomplished fact of Sewall's candidacy with this point: "We must remember that the great masses of the voters in all parties and especially the silver Democrats and silver Republicans whom we hope to gain to our party in the future, care nothing about the Vice-Presidency and would feel bitterly toward any one who put any obstacle in the way of the election of Bryan in this fight." The two most important considerations, according to the Populist chairman, were whether any change would secure more votes for Bryan, and, secondly, how any change might affect the Populist party not only in the campaign but in the future. Perhaps something about the vice presidency more satisfactory to the Populists could be arranged after Bryan's election but before the inauguration.[42]

In addition to Butler's more realistic appraisal of the vice-presidential muddle, the final event that precipitated the completion of electoral fusion in North Carolina was Bryan's visit to the state. Presidential hopefuls of both parties had since the war largely ignored North Carolina, together with the rest of the "solidly" Democratic southern states. But 1896 was different. Several states of the upper South were in doubt. Bryan was not just making a polite courtesy call but giving North Carolina a sample of the "stumping," hitherto unprecedented for presidential candidates, that intrigued the nation.

Most Tarheels, whose real economic interests had long been ignored by the nation's leaders, responded to the Nebraskan with wild enthusiasm. As he boarded the train at Asheville, Bryan's hand was so sore from the thousands of handshakes that he pled, "Be easy, don't squeeze boys!" A man in the pressing crowd yelled back, "Well, just hang your hand out of the window, so we can touch it." A reporter described the scene that followed: "Mr. Bryan cut his eyes around and smiled a broad amiable smile and put his hand out of the window. Then one by one up into the hundreds, the men came and simply touched the back of his hand."

Bryan's greatest qualities, according to the admiring newspaperman, were his "constant remembering of others and his constant forgetfulness of self." Those were the qualities that lay behind "that dignity which was such a gracious dignity—familiar with no one and with which no one was familiar."

[42] Butler to Washburn, September 21, 24, 1896, Campaign Letterbooks, Butler MSS. Butler viewed the bolt of the Gold Democrats as an attempt to insure Bryan's defeat so that they could recapture control of the party. This not only made the continuance of the national Populist organization essential, he believed, but might lead to its absorbing many Bryan Democrats in 1900—if the Gold Democrats should succeed in their designs. Butler to J. M. Patterson, August 28, 1896, *ibid.*

Only the "naturalness of his powers" could explain Bryan's ability to submit to the grueling campaign schedule that he kept, for those men who "looked upon thought as work or mixing with plain people as condescension" would surely break under such strain.[43]

In Raleigh the Democratic state chairman shared the job of presiding at the vast rally for the presidential candidate with the Populist chairman, who introduced Bryan. Behind the scenes Bryan impressed Populist and Democratic leaders alike; one of Butler's lieutenants, after riding on the Bryan Special Train, reported that the presidential candidate talked good Populist doctrine and knew who his true friends were. The time had obviously come for complete and final cooperation on the electoral ticket in North Carolina, and the pro-Bryan parties effected it almost as soon as Bryan left the state.[44]

The arrangement reached by the Populists and Democrats in North Carolina provided for the Democrats to name five Bryan-Sewall electors, the Populists five Bryan-Watson electors, and the National Silver party (Silver Republicans) one Bryan-Sewall elector. Each of the parties was to list its slate of electors, who would be the same on all three tickets, under the party's name. This meant that all of the state's eleven electoral votes would, in the event of the expected victory for national reform, be cast for Bryan; but six of the electors would vote for Sewall for vice president and five of them for Watson.

This was the type of fusion on the electoral ticket that Populists around the nation had been suggesting ever since their convention in St. Louis, and the silver forces in some other states preceded those in North Carolina in effecting the

[43] W. E. Christian, "On the Bryan Special," Raleigh *News and Observer*, September 20, 1896.
[44] James B. Lloyd to Butler, September 19, 1896, Butler MSS; Raleigh *News and Observer*, September 22, 1896.

arrangement. But because of the strategic position and
relative vigor of North Carolina Populism, as well as because
of Marion Butler's key national role, the final completion of
electoral fusion in North Carolina marked a significant
development in the national campaign.

Attacks on the arrangement came from two different extremes. Populist midroaders, of whom North Carolina had
a small but loud share, bitterly fought the plan as a betrayal
of both Tom Watson and the party. The *Progressive Farmer*,
for example, which had diminished in influence since L. L.
Polk's death and the submergence of the Farmers' Alliance
by the People's party, tore into the "cringing politicians" who
had allowed Sewall to remain on the ticket and declared "the
dangerous Maine plutocrat" to be a "warty excrescence on
the body politic" which had to be removed.[45]

On the other hand, conservative, pro-Cleveland Democrats
assailed their party's "sellout" to Populism. In North Carolina, as in other southern states, the National (Gold) Democrats, who had in early September nominated John M. Palmer
of Illinois for the presidency and Simon B. Buckner of
Kentucky for the vice presidency, attracted few followers.
Even those Democrats in the South who sympathized with
the Gold Democrats were reluctant to bolt the "party of good
government and white supremacy." But fusion with "anarchists and socialists," as many hysterical conservatives over
the nation labeled the Populists, was too much. The most
important spokesman for this viewpoint in North Carolina
was the influential Charlotte *Observer*. It promptly donned
the mantle of Democratic super-orthodoxy by insisting that
since Tarheel Democrats regarded the party's national convention as "the supreme court of the party" many of them
now denied the "right of a State Democratic committee to
trade one of the nominees of this convention [Sewall] out of

[45] October 6, 20, 1896.

five of the eleven votes to which he is entitled from North Carolina." Although actually disgusted by the revolution in the Democratic party that had occurred in Chicago, the loyal party organ declared: "Men whose boast is that they have never scratched the Democratic nominee, cannot afford this year to vote for a lot of Populist electors who will vote for a Populist for Vice-President against the Democratic nominee. It is their duty to scratch the name of every Populist from the electoral ticket and to vote only for those men who will vote for the Democratic candidate."[46]

Bryanites among the southern Democrats, such as Josephus Daniels, were both horrified and embarrassed to see party orthodoxy thus carried to its logical extreme. On the other hand, Sewall's alleged "betrayal" by Bryan and Jones inspired false tears in the "goldbug" press of the Northeast. As the fusion plans began to emerge, the New York *Times,* for example, carried a story suggesting that the "pretense that the Democrats have upon their ticket a conservative man of business and property from New England loses its force as an argument in favor of its conservative character when plans have been made which make it impossible that such a man can be elected." The *Times,* like many other eastern newspapers, insisted that since Bryan was actually a Populist in sentiment the fusion arrangement removed "the last possible excuse for any one voting the Bryan-Sewall ticket with the notion that it is a Democratic ticket even in its tail."[47]

Perhaps the most effective answer to the charge that the Democratic nominee for the vice presidency had been betrayed in the fusion scheme came from Sewall himself. In a move designed to lessen the effectiveness of his self-styled "friends," he gave his explicit approval to the union in North Carolina between the Populists and Democrats. "I believe

[46] Quoted in the Raleigh *News and Observer,* September 24, 1896.
[47] August 31, 1896.

the friends of bimetallism ought to vote for the electoral
ticket that will elect Bryan to the Presidency," Sewall
declared in a letter to the Tarheel Democratic chairman, "and
I thoroughly approve of the policy which unites the supporters of free silver in your State and every other." Sewall
hoped that nothing would prevent unity in "the people's
cause against monopolies."[48]

Since Sewall cooperated with the national leadership of his
party while Tom Watson most emphatically and publicly
disagreed with that of the Populists, Butler and his committee
faced special difficulties. Nevertheless, Butler now joined with
Jones in effecting fusion wherever possible. Butler's voluminous correspondence as well as newspaper accounts suggest
that the Populists and Democrats arrived at cooperative
electoral tickets most easily in the critical states of the upper
Midwest. The one exception was Indiana, where fusion was
difficult, and the efforts there will be considered in the
following chapter. But in Minnesota, Michigan, Wisconsin,
Illinois, and Iowa, all crucial and in considerable doubt, the
major reform parties achieved fusion on the electoral ticket
with relative ease.[49]

Within the former Confederate states, only in North

[48] Sewall to Clement Manly, September 29, 1896, in Raleigh *News and
Observer*, October 2, 1896; also New York *Herald*, October 4, 1896. Sewall
had earlier explained, in conjunction with one of his repeated explanations of
why he would not consider withdrawing, that he understood how Bryan
might be elected and he, Sewall, not be. "But I am thinking more of free
silver than of Sewall," he added. "A change in the ticket now is out of the
question." St. Louis *Post-Dispatch*, September 20, 1896.

[49] *Appleton's Annual Cyclopaedia, 1896* (New York, 1897), 770, has a
convenient list of the twenty-eight states where Democrats and Populists
cooperated on the electoral ticket. The division in the states mentioned
above was as follows: Minnesota—4 Democrats, 5 Populists; Michigan—9
Democrats, 4 Populists; Wisconsin—9 Democrats, 3 Populists; Illinois—20
Democrats, 4 Populists; and Iowa—10 Democrats, 3 Populists. Eastern states
which the Bryan forces early conceded to McKinley but where fusion was
effected were: Massachusetts—13 Democrats, 2 Populists; Connecticut—5
Democrats, 1 Populist; New Jersey—9 Democrats, 1 Populist; Pennsylvania—
28 Democrats, 4 Populists; and Ohio—18 Democrats, 5 Populists.

Carolina, Louisiana, and Arkansas were the Democrats and Populists able to come to terms. Electoral fusion failed partly because the Democrats in most of the southern states felt confident of carrying their states without any help from the Populists. But the midroad Populists in the South contributed their influence to blocking fusion too, as in Georgia where the Populists agreed to divide the electoral ticket only if all the Democratic electors would vote for Tom Watson.

Butler used every argument he could devise to strengthen the Populist position in the South. Immediately after agreeing to electoral fusion in North Carolina, he urged Jones to secure the same "winning division of electors" in his own state of Arkansas. Butler pointed out that one of the difficulties in North Carolina had been the Populist fear that in the safely Democratic states of the South the Democrats would not concede anything. He also argued that once he and Jones had gotten their own states safely arranged they would have more influence in achieving fusion in other states. "If there is one State in the Union where you should see that there is a joint electoral ticket," Butler suggested, "it is in your own State. . . . Yet pardon me to say, you should not handicap me in my efforts to give Mr. Bryan the electoral vote in doubtful States, when you could so easily help me by having a division of the electoral vote in your own State." The Populist chairman insisted that Jones had earlier agreed in conversations in Washington to promote Democratic concessions to Populists in the South but whether that actually had been understood or not, Butler concluded, "I insist that it is good politics and I know that it will greatly help me in my work."[50]

Bryan too urged the Arkansas Democrats to make concessions, and when they finally agreed to give the Populists three

[50] Butler to Jones, September 24, 28, 30, 1896, Campaign Letterbooks, Butler MSS.

of the state's eight electors, Butler and Jones tried to use the Arkansas arrangement to inspire fusion in Mississippi.[51] Their efforts failed there, but in Louisiana Butler had earlier been successful in encouraging the Populists to accept the Democratic offer of four of the state's eight electors.[52] In the border states of Kentucky, West Virginia, and Missouri the reform parties also achieved electoral fusion: in Kentucky—11 Democrats, 2 Populists; in West Virginia—4 Democrats, 2 Populists; and in Missouri—13 Democrats, 4 Populists.

Texas, which wound up in the Bryan column in November, proved to be a special headache for Butler. Populism flourished there but, as the national convention had revealed, most of the leaders were extreme midroaders, and there was especially bitter feeling between Populists and Democrats. When the two parties failed to agree on any plan of electoral fusion, the Texas Populists threatened to strike a political bargain that would have been the strangest in a year when many unusual political arrangements were being made: in exchange for Republican support for the Populist state ticket the Populists would vote for McKinley. Presumably this Populist-Republican electoral fusion would allow the Populists to vote for McKinley-Watson electors, though Watson himself repudiated the idea. Clearly the cumbersome electoral college was being used in 1896 in a manner which the Founding Fathers could never have imagined.

Butler coped with Texas as best he could from late August until the end of the campaign. At first he urged the Texas Populist chairman, J. S. Bradley, and Harry Tracy of the *Southern Mercury* to try to get the Democrats to agree on giving the state's fifteen electoral votes to Bryan and Watson. The Populist strategy in the states that were safe for Bryan,

[51] Butler to R. K. Prewitt, October 12, 1896, *ibid.*; New York *Herald*, October 11, 1896.
[52] Butler to A. B. Booth, Populist chairman in Louisiana, September 19, 1896, Campaign Letterbooks, Butler MSS.

Butler explained, was to hold "out stiff to get everything that we possibly can for Watson."[53]

But after Democrats and Populists in Texas failed to reach any agreement and Butler himself had been forced to accept the fact that Sewall was in the race to stay, the Populist national chairman was horrified by the reports that the Texas Populists might aid McKinley in order to hit at the hated Democrats. Ignored by Chairman Bradley, Butler wrote urgently to other Populists in the state; he admitted that the Democrats had acted badly but insisted that no action on their part could possibly justify Populist fusion on the electoral ticket for McKinley. "If our people should foolishly divide the electoral ticket in your State with the gold men," Butler warned, "then you do not only justify the action of the Democrats in your State, to a certain extent, but you would kill the People's party forever in Texas, as well as give it a serious blow all over the country."[54]

The national chairman informed another Texan that when the Populists at St. Louis nominated Bryan they had hoped that Sewall would come down; but, Butler added, there was "no contract made or pledge given by anyone, so far as I know, representing the Democrats, that this would be done, but I think it safe to say that the Convention would have nominated Bryan, anyway, if it had been known distinctly and positively that Sewall would not withdraw, because it was the very best possible thing to do from a party standpoint as well as from a broad and patriotic standpoint." When Hanna's best hope was to create dissensions among the allied silver groups, Butler asked, how could any man who loved his country and believed in the principles of Populism help to defeat a man like Bryan and elect one like McKinley?[55]

[53] Butler to Bradley, August 26, 1896, Butler to Tracy, August 29, 1896, *ibid.*
[54] Butler to M. D. Harrell, October 1, 1896, *ibid.*
[55] Butler to T. J. Middleton, October 12, 1896, *ibid.*

Despite all Butler's letters and warnings, newspaper reports from Texas at the time of the simultaneous meetings of the Republican state convention and the Populist state executive committee continued to mention the possible electoral fusion for McKinley. The deal never came off. One reason why it did not may have been a long telegram from Butler to the Populist chairman that was reported to have knocked the "whole combine to pieces."[56]

Although different from the embarrassment threatened in Texas, trouble for the national leadership of the Populist party also resulted from the situation in Kansas. In most of the western states the Populists secured recognition on the electoral ticket—in Idaho, Montana, Utah, Wyoming, and Washington, all with three or four electoral votes each, the Populists had a fair share. In California they got four of the nine electors, half of the eight in Nebraska, and three of the thirteen in Iowa. In Oregon, all four Bryan electors were pledged to vote for Watson for vice president.[57] But, as mentioned earlier, in Kansas, the western bastion of Populism, the Populists accepted ten Democratic electors in exchange for Democratic support of the entire Populist state ticket. This arrangement, which clearly reflected the Kansas Populists' unconcern for their party's vice-presidential candidate, infuriated not only Tom Watson but Butler and most southern members of the party as well. Shortly after opening campaign headquarters, Butler had warned western Popu-

---

[56] St. Louis *Post-Dispatch*, September 11, 12, 1896. Martin, *People's Party in Texas*, 243, gives figures which suggest that some Populists in Texas went ahead and voted for McKinley in the general election and that many did not vote for any presidential candidate. The Republicans supported the Populist state ticket.

[57] Concerning the Oregon arrangement, Butler had expressed his appreciation and declared: "If all the other states had shown the same nerve and spirit that you have shown we would elect Tom Watson Vice-President beyond question." Butler to W. S. U'ren, August 28, 1896, Campaign Letterbooks, Butler MSS.

lists against trading electors to the Democrats in exchange for support on the state ticket. He insisted that the "strength and dignity of our party will be tested solidly by the run that Watson makes."[58]

Butler informed Senator Jones of the fact that the Kansas arrangement created dissatisfaction among many Populists elsewhere. Midroaders in Kansas, although apparently in a distinct minority, were howling loudly and, after Watson's speeches in the state, planning for their own convention to put out a straight Populist ticket. Butler reminded John W. Breidenthal, Populist chairman in the state, that Populists of the whole country were accustomed to look to Kansas as the "pioneer and bulwark of Populism."[59]

Breidenthal, who was also a member of the Populist national executive committee, explained that he had done all that he could do to secure Watson electors. But the Kansas Populist convention had ignored his advice and made its own decision; he regretted the action, but the time had passed when anything could be done about it. Moreover, Breidenthal argued, Populist control of the Kansas state government, "enabling us to demonstrate what we will do for the people in the way of state legislation," and the election of six straight Populist congressmen plus a Populist United States senator were sufficiently important to make the national committee think twice before attempting to upset the arrangement.[60]

Despite Breidenthal's defense of the Kansas fusion, Butler

[58] Butler to Harry D. Moore, a Populist leader in Montana, August 31, 1896, *ibid.*

[59] Butler to Jones, September 7, 1896, and Butler to Breidenthal, September 7, 1896, *ibid.* Butler was wary, however, of the midroad faction and warned that the national committee "would not advise anything which would tend to help the election of Mr. McKinley, even though the situation was not satisfactory from a People's party standpoint." Butler to Abe Steinberger, August 29, 1896, *ibid.*

[60] Breidenthal to Butler, September 14, 21, 1896, Butler MSS.

persevered in his efforts to find some way to have the electors divided between Sewall and Watson. He suggested at one point that he would persuade Jones to get Kansas Democrats to divide the electors if the Populists would give the nomination for chief justice to a Democrat and both parties would support a Silver Republican for congressman-at-large. Although he refused to work with the Kansas midroaders, whom Breidenthal and other Kansas Populists accused of being secretly allied with the Republicans, Butler was never able to change the one-sided electoral ticket in Kansas.[61]

As Tom Watson grew increasingly uncontrollable and antagonistic to the national committee's policy, Butler finally took this position toward the Kansas situation: "I cannot approve, as I have said, of the arrangement which our people have made in Kansas, but in as much as nothing in that state would satisfy Mr. Watson but all of the electors, neither will I approve of endorsing the bolting electoral ticket [of the midroaders], which can have no other purpose or result but to turn over that state to McKinley. There has never been but one chance of electing Watson Vice President, which was to get Sewall to withdraw. I fear that Watson's conduct has made this impossible. Then why should we jeopardize the state of Kansas, not only giving the electoral vote to McKinley, but also defeating six People's party Congressmen in that state, as well as a United States Senator, in return for nothing?" The national committee would just have to keep its "hands off" the Kansas situation and have nothing to do with Watson's "little spite game of his own."[62]

[61] Butler to Breidenthal, September 12, 21, 1896, Campaign Letterbooks, Butler MSS.

[62] Butler to Washburn, October 3, 1896, *ibid.* Butler also had a problem about Colorado's three electors, all pledged to Sewall, but it did not create as much resentment and attract nationwide attention as did the Kansas matter. See Butler to T. M. Patterson, September 1, 1896, *ibid.*, where Butler appealed to the Coloradan's "sense of fairness and right" and

Despite vexatious problems in Kansas, Texas, and elsewhere, Butler and his Populist associates threw themselves energetically into the campaign. Fusion had "taken" in more states than it had failed in, and the unprecedented exertions of Bryan, together with his personal magnetism, seemed to fire the loyalty and admiration of those Populist leaders who worked with him. Ignatius Donnelly, for example, left the St. Louis convention dispirited and unhappy. He had finally, after much vacillation and collaboration with the extreme midroaders, swung around to support the nomination of Watson and Bryan, but his heart was not in the campaign. Stung by the Minnesota Populists' failure to support his own candidacy at St. Louis, Donnelly published a personal and emotional statement in his newspaper proclaiming that he was "weary of this whole business" of politics and would, after the campaign, retire to his library.[63]

But the popular orator was soon deeply engaged in Bryan's behalf. Donnelly went to Lincoln to speak at the Silver Republicans' notification meeting for Bryan. "From 4 to 6 I slept, accumulating electricity, like a torpedo eel," Donnelly recorded in his diary, "for the meeting to-night." Then he spoke for over two hours to a crowd gathered before the hotel and estimated at from five to seven thousand persons. "I was pleased & proud to observe that after talking for over 2 hours, in the open air, at 64 years of age, I was as fresh as when I started," Donnelly noted. As for Bryan, Donnelly believed that the Nebraskan was "a very able, shrewd, wise man."

---

reminded him of the party's sectional bargain at St. Louis. Patterson replied that with half of the Colorado Populists the question was not one of party but of the remonetization of silver and that it would have been impossible to have the state's Populist convention endorse Watson. Patterson to Butler, September 17, 1896, *ibid.*

[63] The piece is pasted in his diary for 1896 as well as in his scrapbook, Donnelly MSS, Minnesota Historical Society; see also Ridge, *Ignatius Donnelly*, 357.

And after both Bryan and his wife had finished flattering him during dinner, Donnelly speculated: "I have a dim hope that I may perchance get a seat in his cabinet if he is elected —but I have been disappointed so often that I am not sanguine as to any thing."[64]

The more he labored for and with Bryan the greater Donnelly's zeal grew. A month after his initial encounter with Bryan during the campaign, Donnelly shared a vast crowd with the presidential candidate in St. Paul. The next day he called on Bryan and "his bright-faced, keen-minded little wife." Bryan invited him into a bedroom where the tired candidate rested. Donnelly showed Bryan a letter from Butler and a copy of one of Butler's appeals to Tom Watson. The diary entry continued: "We talked over the whole situation; and then Mr. Bryan proceeded to tell me what he proposed to do if elected president. His purposes are pure and noble. He is a great man; and if he is the choice of the people he will give the country an administration the greatest and best it has ever enjoyed. It seems to me he has been raised up by Providence to save the country from sinking into old world conditions."[65]

Just as Donnelly's admiration increased for the candidate that many Populists had accepted reluctantly, so did Marion Butler's. He had, since the St. Louis convention, constantly emphasized the fact that Bryan was just as much the nominee of the Populists as of the Democrats, and Butler, in all his correspondence and public statements, had stressed Bryan's suitability for the role. But during the midst of the campaign,

[64] Entry for September 7-9, diary for 1896, Donnelly MSS. Describing a successful speech to 10,000 persons on October 7, Donnelly observed that he found that a tablespoonful of whiskey "just before speaking" helped "not only by warming up the intellect, but by helping digestion & preventing the formation of gases in the stomach. . . . As I use stimulants at no other time a very little has great effect upon me."

[65] Entry for October 10-11, *ibid.*

and after a personal encounter with the Nebraskan, the Populist chairman seemed to acquire a deeper regard for Bryan. After the peripatetic candidate passed through Washington on his way to address "laboring men" in Brooklyn, Butler had some striking advice for Senator Jones about "our candidate for President."

First of all, Butler believed that Bryan should not let the eagerness of people to see and hear him draw him into making too many speeches in one day. His strength could not hold out unless he took better care of himself. And even if he spoke a dozen times a day only a small percentage of the people could hear him; if he only made one speech a day it would be reported more connectedly in the great dailies and put before the voters of the whole country.[66]

The Populist chairman further suggested that the Democratic national committee, which even though its own funds were limited still had more than the Populists did, should send a manager along with Bryan to arrange all the numerous details "which must be very fatiguing and annoying to a man in Mr. Bryan's position." Local committees not only did not help the harassed candidate but often were a nuisance. Butler continued with a description that suggests the almost primitive quality of Bryan's determined bid for the presidency: "Last night, Mr. Bryan was forced to look up the schedule from here to Dover, [Delaware] in order to reach there by the regular train. He was forced to leave here and go part of the way, stop in the middle of the night, get up

[66] The fallacy in Butler's argument here was that many large dailies, such as the New York *Evening Post* and Hartford *Courant*, made no bones about a policy of not giving coverage to "heresy" and "fanaticism." The *Post* argued that there was not and should not be a place in any intelligent newspaper, even in the news columns, for the Bryanites' "yawps of ignorance and folly." The New York *Times*, of which Chattanooga's Adolph S. Ochs became publisher and general manager in August 1896, dissented from this view in an editorial on October 25, 1896. But even the *Times'* news columns were far from objective.

early this morning at six o'clock, catch another train in order
to catch a local train going to his place of speaking. If he had
had a manager, he could have rested here during the night,
left this morning and had a special train over the branch
route of 20 or 25 miles that would have taken him directly
to his speaking place. The newspaper men who are traveling
with him, tell me that things of this kind are constantly
occurring. You may have considered all these matters before,
but it seems to me that our candidate for President should
not be forced to look after such annoying details. One of the
newspaper men told me that Mr. Bryan has often been
forced to carry his heavy grips from the train some distance
up the street; that in one place he was forced to walk from
the train up town, no arrangements having been made to have
a carriage for him. Mr. Bryan may not object to any of these
things but yet I do not think it should be allowed."[67] Despite
the campaign's hardships that Butler described, Bryan continued to evoke powerful responses, not only from the thousands who heard his speeches but from individuals who found
themselves caught up in the first genuinely exciting and meaningful presidential election in several decades.

Henry Demarest Lloyd was not, however, one of those individuals. Finally realizing that the great bulk of the Populists were not interested in doctrinaire socialism, Lloyd retired
to his summer home in Rhode Island and more or less
washed his hands of the whole business. When a small group
of the disgruntled midroad Populists in Chicago bolted and
named Lloyd as their candidate for lieutenant-governor, Florence Kelley gave him the news. A prominent associate of
Jane Addams and Governor Altgeld's appointee as Illinois
factory inspector, she wrote Lloyd: "I wonder whether any
candid friend has told you that the disreputable end of the

[67] Butler to Jones, September 21, 1896, Campaign Letterbooks, Butler MSS.

Populists have nominated you and are using your name for Lieutenant-Governor."[68]

Although Lloyd refused to allow the midroaders to use his name on their ticket, he sympathized with their views and remained aloof from the struggle that Florence Kelley regarded as so desperate. When Lloyd publicly derided the silver issue in a speech towards the end of the campaign, the president of the United Brotherhood of Carpenters and Joiners of America wrote that he had been "grieved" to hear Lloyd talk. "We may not think the question deserves all the attention it is now receiving," the labor leader declared, "but the other parts of the platform are o. k. and again this is a fight in which the people are against the organized Plutocrats of the country. . . . Let us hope that the people's Champion will *Win*."[69]

Lloyd could remain coolly detached, but his sister found it impossible to remain dispassionate about the question that most Americans were excited about. Herself an intellectual person who kept up a lively correspondence with her brother and knew his political views, Caro Lloyd Withington finally confessed: "We illuminated last evening for the Bryan local parade, and we hung out Grandpa Lloyd's enormous big flag with 26 stars. I couldn't resist putting 'Bryan & Sewall' on the edge of our little flag to help on the cause. I can't vote you see. I have wanted to vote so in this election, that I positively have had a feeling of humiliation that I couldn't."

[68] Florence Kelley to Lloyd, October 1, 1896, Lloyd MSS. Much involved in Altgeld's bid for reelection, Florence Kelley bemoaned Lloyd's absence: "We miss you very much in the campaign. Things are badly muddled, and Governor Altgeld's friends seem few, indeed, in this time of need. The Socialists and the laborskates are kicking him alike. The Silver Populists and the straight trades-union vote seem to be his main hope besides the farmers. And if the working people allow him to be defeated now, in the face of his record, surely they deserve to have no other friend until this generation dies out and another and better one takes its place."
[69] H. Lloyd of Boston to Henry D. Lloyd, November 1, 1896, *ibid.*

Mrs. Withington added that the Bryan club in her home of Belleville, New Jersey, had more than double the membership of the McKinley club but the Bryanites were "not found in our section of the town."[70]

When Bryan and silver aroused such enthusiasm in a New Jersey town, one can imagine the political atmosphere in a bustling, Democratic stronghold like Atlanta. There the *Constitution* reported that everyone was wearing campaign buttons; while mostly they were said to bear Bryan's likeness, some astute traveling salesmen were equipped with revolving buttons that carried pictures of all the candidates so that no customer would be offended. Bryan's "soft alpine hat with the stiff brim" had become the rage and was expected to be the "predominating headgear among the members of the general assembly this year."

A reporter found the Kimball House lobby and corridors seething with "political agitation." Even the men lined up in front of the bar were drinking "silver fizzes." The bartender confided: "Strange, I've had a huge run on campaign drinks this season. It's that way all over the country. I got a letter from a friend of mine who runs a hotel bar in Cincinnati. . . . Just a little Holland gin with the white of an egg stirred in, and you have the silver fizz. Put in the yolk and you have a mixture done up to the royal taste of Hanna and the gold crowd."

One newly elected legislator from south Georgia inadvertently illustrated the mood of the rural majority of Americans. He strolled into the Kimball House with "a wire-grass smile on his honest face and a rural splice in his coat which proved that he represented the struggling masses." He stopped near the "graphophone" that stood by one of the walnut pillars and began to examine with awe the machine and its varied repertoire. Finally he inserted his nickel, cranked past

---

[70] Caro L. Withington to Lloyd, November 1, 1896, *ibid.*

"Just Tell Them that You Saw Me" and a cornet solo, and selected a recording of Bryan's "Cross of Gold" speech.

Placing the tubing to his ear, the Georgia Cracker refused to allow the machine's nasal tone to diminish his enjoyment and began to "gesticulate with his loose arm." Finally as Bryan reached his peroration about the cross of gold: "There was a sudden yell through the corridor, which caused the dust to fall from the skylight above. The man from the wiregrass gave a spontaneous shout, 'Hurrah for Bryan.' The cheer was taken up, and for several minutes the lobby resounded with shouts for Bryan."[71]

Shouts and hurrahs would not, of course, elect Bryan president. But by October, as the campaign entered its final phase, the Populist leaders had consolidated their ranks to a surprising degree and were determined to contribute what they could to the great allied bid for reform. Disgruntled midroaders continued to protest and threaten, Tom Watson chief among them, but most of the rank and file and virtually all of the leaders saw, as one Wisconsin Populist put it, "the folly of kicking during the battle."[72]

[71] Atlanta *Constitution*, October 3, 16, 1896.
[72] C. W. Staples to Ignatius Donnelly, August 14, 1896, Donnelly MSS.

4

The Campaign: Final Phase

DESPITE the initial confusion about notification caused by Butler's ambiguous statement to the press, the Populists did notify their candidates in 1896 by letters, as had been done in 1892. Bryan and Watson, each in his own fashion, also accepted the nominations by letter.[1]

Senator William V. Allen of Nebraska, as permanent chairman of the Populists' St. Louis convention, headed the committee to notify Bryan. Butler insisted that the letters of notification be sent not later than September 15 and that the one to Bryan precede or at least go simultaneously with the one to Watson. "Our people have gotten so worked up over this matter of notification," Butler confessed, "that we cannot get them to think of anything else until this matter is definitely settled. The quicker it is adjusted and over with, the better for Mr. Bryan and for us."[2]

In Allen's letter of September 15, 1896, he explained first that the Populists had taken the liberty of nominating Bryan without consulting him because they considered it their patriotic duty to bring about a "union of all reform forces" and because "the money question is the overshadowing political issue of the age." Allen continued: "It has at no time been expected, nor is it now, that you will abandon your adhesion to the Chicago platform, nor that you will accept all that is declared in the People's party platform, however gratifying the latter would be to all Populists. It must be understood that the party does not abate one jot or tittle of loyalty to its principles. We have declared ourselves in favor of many important reforms, and go farther than you or your party have gone. These reforms are, in our judgment, essential to the liberation of the people from present unjust and iniquitous industrial bondage."

Allen and his committee assured Bryan that the Populists would exact from him no promises other than "those made in your public utterances and exemplified in a life devoted to the welfare" of the human race, nor would they ask him to abandon the Democratic party. Rising above "mere partisan surroundings," the Populists believed Bryan highly qualified to bring about reform "in a way that will work injury to none and [give] justice to all, thus making our Government in fact, as it is now in form only, a government 'of, by and for the people.' "[3]

Bryan's reply began with the declaration that the honor had been tendered him "in such a generous spirit and upon such honorable terms" that he was able to accept the Populist nomination without departing from the Democratic platform. After lauding the Populists' "breadth of patriotism" which led them to sacrifice partisan advantage for the sake of union among reformers, Bryan alluded to the problems inherent in fusion: "While difficulties always arise in the settlement of the details of any plan of co-operation between distinct political organizations, I am sure that the friends who are working towards a common result always find it possible to agree upon just and equitable terms. The American people have proven equal to every emergency which has arisen in the past, and I am confident that in the present emergency there

[1] Hicks, *Populist Revolt*, 369, erroneously states that no notifications were made and that Bryan never accepted or rejected the Populist nomination.
[2] Butler to Allen, September 5, 1896, Campaign Letterbooks, Butler MSS.
[3] New York *Times*, September 15, 1896; also *Bryan, First Battle*, 430-31.

will be no antagonism between the various divisions of the one great body which is marching to repel an invasion more dangerous to our welfare than an army with banners."[4]

The gamble in nominating Bryan that the Populists had taken in late July had finally come out all right. They had known full well, from the newspapers and General Weaver's speech, that Bryan did not wish the delegates at St. Louis to nominate him unless they also named Sewall. Yet in the clear light of this knowledge the Populists had done what they knew they had to do if they wished to remain a national party with a western as well as a southern wing. The alternative of nominating a Populist, or any candidate other than Bryan, would have effectively destroyed the party in the West and seriously weakened it in much of the South.

In accepting the Populist nomination, moreover, Bryan was not necessarily acting purely in the ̄interests of the Democratic party. As mentioned earlier, Governor Stone of Missouri, an influential spokesman for the Democrats, urged Bryan to avoid the complications that arose from having the two vice-presidential candidates by tactfully declining the Populist nomination. Some Democratic newspapers, such as the Mobile *Register*, took the same line. And if Bryan had wished to destroy the People's party as a factor in national politics, the course urged by Governor Stone probably would have been the quickest and surest way to do it. To destroy Populism was not, however, Bryan's aim.

His willingness to accept the embarrassment connected with having two running mates and his absolute self-restraint in the face of the increasingly bitter things said by some midroad Populists suggest that Bryan too, like the Populist majority, had in a sense "put principle above party" so that the election of 1896 would find reformers welded together in their great bid for a change. Fusion between the Democrats

---

[4] New York *Herald*, October 4, 1896; Bryan, *First Battle*, 432-33.

and Populists was not, in other words, the simple matter of Democratic gain and Populist sacrifice that many historians have depicted.

Tom Watson, however, saw the whole thing in his own peculiar way and remained impenetrable to the slightest suggestion that he might be wrong. The Democrats, he was sure, wanted to "play whale to the Populists' Jonah." He thought there was nothing else to be said. Marion Butler, in his letter officially notifying Watson of the St. Louis convention's nomination, steered clear of Watson's extremism but took a more partisan stance than Senator Allen had in the letter to Bryan. After a long sketch of the economic and political conditions that had given rise to the People's party, Butler claimed that it was the first party in a generation to make "an honest demand for the free and unrestricted coinage of silver" and also, among other things, the first party to "make definite and specific what is meant by opposition to monopolies, instead of indulging in glittering generalities."

The Populist chairman developed the thesis that he had touched on in his keynote address at St. Louis: the Populists had driven the Democrats to make the sharp turn towards reform that they had made in their Chicago convention, and it was the People's party that held the older party to the proper course. If the Populists should be eliminated, "the evil and blighting influences that have dominated and corrupted the Democratic party in the past would creep into its council and control it again."

When he came to the matter of Bryan's running mate, Butler ignored the Populists' internal division that had inspired the nomination of their own vice-presidential candidate and indirectly attacked, without naming, Sewall. Bryan was "a man who was ready to renounce the false gods of a corrupted Democracy," Butler declared. But when the Democrats failed to be "true to the people" and to their platform and named for the vice presidency a man whose past was "obscured in a silence suggestive of either ignorance or indifference to the struggle of the people with the money power," the Populists had been forced to nominate independently. In doing so, Butler concluded, the Populists had found a "man worthy to have headed the ticket" and a "man who represents what Mr. Bryan represents." The Bryan-Watson ticket, in short, was "not only the best silver ticket" but "the true co-operative ticket."[5]

More than these flattering words were needed to placate Watson, for at the time that Butler's letter appeared in the newspapers the Georgian was pouring out his anti-Sewall version of electoral cooperation to a series of audiences in the West and feeding the resentment of the midroaders. Watson opened his tour with an address to about 5,000 Texans in Dallas. Although he asked his cheering followers to stand by Bryan, the dispatches of the press associations that appeared in newspapers across the country emphasized Watson's fulminations against Sewall. Disharmony in the camp of the silverites made good copy, and Watson's speeches now proved to be a never-failing source of news. Claiming to be the true disciple of Populism, the Georgian insisted that, "so long as Tom Watson lives the People's Party shall not die."[6] "You must burn the bridges if you follow me," Watson proclaimed. "I am for straight Populism (cheers) and I do not propose to be carried to one side of the road or the other (wild cheering)." Bryan and Watson, he asserted, would speak for the masses while Sewall talked for the banks and railroads.[7]

Reactions varied to Watson's first major speaking appear-

[5] New York *Times*, September 15, 1896.
[6] New York *Times*, September 8, 1896.
[7] Dallas *Morning News*, September 8, 1896, and *People's Party Paper*, September 8, 1896, as quoted in Woodward, *Watson*, 319-20.

ance in the national campaign. Reed, traveling with Watson as the representative of the Populist national committee, reported to Butler that he and Watson had found Texas ripe for revolt against any fusion with the Democrats that would involve Sewall's remaining in the race. As for the reports about Populist cooperation with Republicans in Texas on some sort of McKinley-Watson ticket, Watson believed that he had successfully checked that for the time being. "Tom may not follow the course always that seems best to us," Reed commented, "but it seems to me that he possesses the genius of patriotism & true statesmanship in an unusual degree."[8]

Loyal Democrats viewed Watson's campaign debut in a quite different light. The pro-Bryan St. Louis *Post-Dispatch* declared editorially that, "Tom Watson has thrown off the mask" and "declared himself the Judas of this campaign." The *Post-Dispatch*, which thought that Watson rather than Sewall had a patriotic duty to withdraw from the race, asserted: "No one who reads Watson's attack upon Sewall, his exaltation of himself, and his assertion that if Watson is defeated Bryan shall be defeated, can doubt what his purpose is. . . . If he is not on the pay roll of the Consolidated Hanna Trust, he is not getting his due. For no man is working harder for that Trust than Tom Watson of Georgia."[9]

The sardonic amusement of the eastern newspapers about the Watson-Sewall imbroglio is well illustrated by the New York *Times'* editorial declaration that there was "more sense and pertinence, together with boundless impertinence, in half a column of Tom than in a page and half of Bryan." The *Times* suggested that Watson actually did represent the voting strength of the "Popocrat" Bryan more accurately than did Sewall. After all, "Sewall is a man of some social and

[8] Reed to Butler, September 7, 1896, Butler MSS.
[9] St. Louis *Post-Dispatch*, September 8, 1896.

commercial standing, and is reasonably suspected of changing his linen three times a week."[10]

Bryan, when shown a copy of Watson's speech, would only say, "I do not care to discuss it." Butler employed the same tactic that he had used earlier in connection with Senator Jones' slur on the southern Populists: "I am not ready to believe that Mr. Watson was quoted correctly as saying that Bryan would be defeated if Sewall was not taken down from the ticket. Certainly he meant to make no threat, as this newspaper report would seem to imply." Butler went on to explain that Democrats had made a mistake in nominating Sewall and that Sewall's duty was clearly to "remove this friction" from the campaign. But whether Sewall took the high road or not, the Populist chairman insisted that "the People's Party can be depended upon to defeat the monopolists and goldbugs in this fight, if it is in its power so to do."[11]

In a private letter to the Populist vice-presidential candidate, Butler spoke as diplomatically as he could: "Allow me to suggest that you be careful to say nothing in your speeches that can possibly be construed into a threat. That is, we cannot afford to say anything which can be construed either directly or indirectly as a threat that Bryan shall be defeated and McKinley elected if the Democratic managers should fail to take down Mr. Sewall." Butler, a champion of the indirect approach, agreed that the Populists should push the Bryan-Watson ticket as the truly cooperative one and the best silver ticket, but the job should be done in a manner best calculated to win support from Silver Republicans and even from Democrats. The chairman's view was that direct, personal attacks on Sewall merely gave him popular sympathy that he did not deserve. "In short, you have it in your power," Butler

[10] New York *Times*, September 9, 1896. The *Times* printed another editorial on September 11 about Watson's attack on Sewall in the weekly journal, the *Independent*.
[11] New York *Times*, September 8, 1896.

pled to Watson, "to do more for the building up of your party, and more for insuring the defeat of the gold men and monopolies in this fight than any other man. . . . I beg you in the interests of our party, and in the interests of suffering humanity to consider well these matters, and have them in view with every public utterance that you make."[12]

Before he could have received Butler's letter, Watson proceeded to Kansas, where the sentiment among the majority of Populists differed greatly from that in Texas, as the fusion arrangement in Kansas clearly reflected. In Abilene, Watson was quoted as saying: "You must be for me or for Sewall, there is no middle ground. I stopped the fusion of the Populists in the South, and propose to stop it in the North. You cannot afford to trade the national ticket for local spoils." Midroaders in Kansas were delighted, one of them declaring to Butler that the Kansas Populist leaders had sold the party out "soul and body" to the Democrats whereas the members *"love* Watson and hate Democrats, & their wholesale slaughter of the Party & our fearless leader of the South will be resented in a way that all may understand it."[13]

Even Reed, however, admitted that he and Watson had "met with some coldness" in their reception in Kansas, though Watson was orator enough to warm up his audiences once he got started with them. Regardless of Watson's oratory, most Kansas Populists must have felt like the county chairman who admitted his bafflement to Butler. Describing himself as an admirer of Watson, this Kansan said that he had switched over to supporting fusion with the Democrats in the state when the Republicans had made their opposition to it blatant. He believed that those midroaders who were calling for a bolting convention were really working for the

[12] Butler to Watson, September 8, 1896, loose copy in Butler MSS and one also in Campaign Letterbooks.
[13] St. Louis *Post-Dispatch*, September 12, 1896; J. F. Willets, a national lecturer for the Farmers' Alliance, to Butler, September 9, 1896, Butler MSS.

Republicans. Perhaps Watson's "indefensible" speeches reflected his ignorance of the true situation in Kansas, but why
had he not consulted Senator Peffer or Jerry Simpson, "who
have gone through as much or more than he has for this
cause"? The Kansan concluded that perhaps Watson's "sectional background" was too different and kept him from taking a broad enough view of things.[14]

Either Watson had received and heeded Butler's private
counsel by the time he reached Lincoln, Nebraska, or else the
intensely pro-Bryan atmosphere there inspired a more moderate approach. Watson and Reed both admired Butler's letter
of notification, and that may have placated him. At any rate,
his speech in Lincoln contained no reference to Sewall nor to
the Republicans' sweeping victory in the Maine election.
Instead, with Mrs. Bryan sitting in one of the boxes on the
side of the hall, the Georgian warmly praised Nebraska's
presidential candidate and emphasized his own intention to
stand firm in the common fight for reform. Reed considered
the speech a great one and felt pleased that Watson had
shown that he was not the "rantankerous cuss" that so many
people thought. James H. Edmisten, the Populist chairman
in Nebraska, informed Butler that the speech was one of the
finest ever made in the state.[15]

Butler, no doubt vastly relieved at the new turn in Watson's
course, congratulated him on the fine impression that the
"masterly" speech in Lincoln had made and reported that it

[14] Reed to Butler, September 10, 1896, Henry McLean, Populist chairman
of Marion County, Kansas, to Butler, September 16, 1896, Butler MSS.
The state chairman of Iowa said that they could use Watson in the state
"upon the condition that he in no wise touches upon the situation as regards
the vice-presidential candidate." Good Populist doctrine "without reference
to any personal matters and without attacking" the Democrats would be
fine. J. Bellangee to Butler, September 11, 1896, *ibid.*

[15] Atlanta *Constitution*, September 17, 1896; Reed to Butler, September
16, 1896, Butler to Washburn, September 18, 1896, Campaign Letterbooks,
Butler MSS.

was being printed as a campaign document. Since there were twice as many requests for Watson to speak as he could possibly accept, Butler asked the Georgian to indicate his preferences. The chairman also reported that the Populists' campaign handbook was about ready to roll off the presses but was being held for Watson's letter of acceptance.[16]

Butler's satisfaction about Watson's role was short lived, and despite Watson's pleasure about the letter of notification his own letter of acceptance was a long way in the future. The Georgian had only temporarily subsided and had by no means changed his desire to be the vice-presidential candidate of the Democrats as well as of the Populists. With the silver parties in several important states, especially Missouri and Indiana, then engaged in negotiations about electoral fusion, harmony among Populist spokesmen was highly desirable. George F. Washburn, the Populist committeeman in charge of the Chicago headquarters, and M. C. Rankin, an Indianian and treasurer of the Populist national committee, traveled to St. Louis to meet Watson and Reed as they returned from the West. Although rumors and misinformation about the conference filled the newspapers, Watson would only say that he had told the Texas Populists that he "would be ashamed to take a single vote that was not given to Bryan as well." "I am for Bryan and Watson," he declared. "I want free silver to win, and at the same time I want to preserve the party organization. We have other reform questions which must be taken up and settled."[17]

[16] Butler to Watson, September 22, 1896, Campaign Letterbooks, Butler MSS.

[17] St. Louis *Post-Dispatch*, September 22, 1896. In a hotel across the street from the one where the Populist leaders conferred, the president of the American Bankers' Association ended his annual address to the convention then meeting in St. Louis: "Solemnly, with a fervor and honesty of purpose that were evidenced by closed eyes and reverent posture, [he concluded], 'From the folly of free silverites, from dishonesty and repudiation, from Anarchy and ruin, O Lord, deliver us.' " *Ibid.*

Butler eagerly awaited word about the conference at St.
Louis. He pressed Washburn for information: "I am anxious
to know the result of your interview with Watson. How has
the Western situation impressed him? Has it toned him down
any, and what line do you think he will proceed on when he
takes the stump again?" Butler agreed with Washburn that
"the chief thing for us to do in this campaign, as far as party
interests are concerned, is to make every move we can to
strengthen our party in the future, and the way to do so is to
show a greater desire to win a victory for silver than anybody
else shows." Watson was in the position to do the Populist
party the greatest good—or damage—but he seemed "to have
overlooked this view of the situation entirely." Butler argued
that, "The people that we must yet win to our party care
nothing about his individuality, or your individuality or mine,
or for any of our personal grievances."[18]

Now deeply involved in the negotiations for electoral
fusion in several states, Butler felt great relief when Reed
came to Washington and reported, according to Butler's
account, that Watson was "now ready to agree that the
course the committee has pursued is best, and, beside, he will
not mention the Vice-Presidential matter in any of his other
speeches." In what must have been one of his few bright
moments during the campaign, Butler happily counted on
Watson's help in impressing the American voters that the
People's party was more willing to make sacrifices for the
success of reform than any other group was. Watson, making
speeches that put Bryan first, could spend October in Indiana,
Illinois, Michigan, Minnesota, and Iowa. "In fact, the battle
is to be won or lost in these States," Butler argued. Bryan
should be sent to concentrate his efforts there. Then if
"Watson makes the same kind of speeches that he can make,

[18] Butler to Washburn, September 24, 1896, Campaign Letterbooks,
Butler MSS.

and that Mr. Reed now says he will make, when he gets out there and gets into the campaign, he will be almost as much of a drawing-card as Bryan himself." Why, Watson could help Bryan "carry the doubtful states and save the fight."[19]

Whether or not the elusive Watson actually had agreed at St. Louis to follow a course more in harmony with that of Butler and the national executive committee is uncertain. Several of the participants in the conference clearly thought that at least he had consented not to lend active support to midroaders who were fighting fusion in the critical states. In Indiana the midroad Populists insisted that all of the fusion electors should be pledged to Watson. Paul Vandervoort, a midroader from Nebraska who was a former Republican and prominent in the Grand Army of the Republic, visited Indiana and other close states to encourage the Populist opponents of fusion.

Butler confessed his bewilderment about Vandervoort, who had no connection with the Populist national committee and whose efforts controverted those of the national leaders. "He certainly has an unusual amount of patriotism and more private funds to spare than most of us," Butler wrote to Rankin of Indiana, "if he can take it upon himself as an individual to go from Nebraska to your state to take a hand in your politics." Nebraska Populist leaders issued a statement characterizing Vandervoort as "a traitor, whose sole object is to defeat Bryan" and as a "Hannacrat" whose "reputation for twenty years has been that of a railroad capper around the Nebraska legislatures."

When Vandervoort appealed to Butler to repudiate the statement of the Nebraska Populists, Butler replied that they knew the facts better than he did and that he could hardly repudiate the statement unless he knew it to be untrue. To Vandervoort's point that he had traveled through Indiana

[19] Butler to Washburn, September 28, 1896, *ibid.*

and other states merely to advance the interests of the Populist party and Tom Watson, Butler responded that he might well have checked with the party's national headquarters before spending so much money and time in advocating a policy that the national leadership did not support. "It must be remembered that the People's Party has candidates for President and Vice-President," Butler added. "Therefore, any man who attempts to advance the interests of Mr. Watson at the expense of Mr. Bryan is, whether he is conscious of it or not, acting against the interests of both and in the interests of McKinley and the gold standard."[20]

To counter the work of Vandervoort, M. C. Rankin returned to Indiana from the meeting with Watson and the others in St. Louis and reported that both the national committee and Watson approved of the Indiana Populists' acceptance of electoral fusion with the Democrats. Although Watson promptly telegraphed his disavowal of this position to Indiana midroaders, the Populist committee voted eleven to one in favor of accepting the Democratic offer of five of the state's fifteen electors. This meant that there was still a good chance for the completion of fusion in the last of the most closely contested states in the nation.[21]

[20] Butler to Rankin, September 21, 1896, Butler to Vandervoort, September 22, 1896, *ibid.*

[21] St. Louis *Post-Dispatch,* September 17-30, 1896; Atlanta *Constitution,* September 26-30, 1896. In Missouri too Vandervoort and the midroaders failed to thwart the electoral fusion of the Populists and Democrats. When Watson denied that he had known anything about the Missouri arrangement, the chairman of that state's Populists declared: "When Watson went through St. Louis on his way to Georgia from Kansas, I met him at the Southern Hotel. The sole object of my call was to tell him what had been proposed in Missouri and what we were going to do. I told him that the sub-committee of the Populist committee had agreed that four [out of seventeen] electors were all the party were entitled to, or could get, and that fusion would be arranged on that basis." The Missouri Populist leader insisted that Watson "did not oppose it, and was fully informed as to every detail." Watson, he concluded, evidently wanted to disrupt the Populist party in every state where fusion had been arranged, and "the purpose in

Watson might have had a temporary change of mind from the time that he made the widely praised speech in Lincoln, Nebraska, until after the conference at St. Louis. But by the end of September he apparently had decided to cut loose and publicly go on the warpath against Butler and the national committee. Not only had North Carolina Populists finally agreed to fusion on September 21, but Bryan had proceeded up the East coast after his speeches in North Carolina and was enjoying a much needed rest at Sewall's home in Bath, Maine.

Watson exploded. "Your deal in North Carolina," he announced to Butler, "is as indefensible as those in Kansas and Colorado." According to Watson, Butler had forced fusion where the Democrats needed Populist votes and not demanded it in Kansas and Colorado where "they had annihilated our party." "Your course is not only ruinous to the interests of the party you were chosen to represent," Watson declared, "but ruinous to Mr. Bryan also. You cannot deliver the Populist vote, as per your fusion deals with the Sewall men."[22]

Not content with his private blast, Watson again favored the New York *World* with an exclusive story in the form of advance sheets of an editorial that he had written for his *People's Party Paper*. This time Watson, in what the *World* played up as the "most important political utterance of the campaign," assailed not Sewall but the policy of the Populist national executive committee. The Georgian declared that Bryan's success was endangered by "the profound dissatisfaction which exists among the humble, honest, earnest Populists who have built up the People's party." Ironically, in view of his own apparent interest in the vice presidency, Watson

doing that could only be to promote the election of the Republican candidate for President." St. Louis *Post-Dispatch*, October 19, 1896.

[22] Watson to Butler, September 27, 1896, Butler MSS.

avowed that deep in the hearts of men "who want no office and hunger for no pie, is settling the conviction that they have been tricked, sold out, betrayed, misled." "If McKinley is elected," he concluded, "the responsibility will forever rest upon those managers who had it in their power to control by fair means 2,000,000 [Populist] votes and lost them by violating the terms of the compact."[23]

The Populist national chairman's optimism about the course of his party's vice-presidential candidate now collapsed almost as soon as it had risen. While newspapers over the nation gave front page coverage to Watson's declaration of war on his own party's leadership, Butler revealed his distress in private letters and refused to make any statement for reporters. To Reed, who had so recently brought hopeful tidings, Butler declared that Watson seemed determined to "pursue his own course, regardless of whatever you and I might agree upon, and, I might say, regardless of the consequences." The chairman reminded Reed, his colleague on the Populist national executive committee, that when the committee met in August to organize and plan for the campaign there had been a choice of two courses of action.

One was for the Populists to insist that there would be no fusion electoral tickets in any state as long as Sewall remained in the race. Butler continued: "In the first place, a number of our Western states would not have stood by us in such a position. Therefore, we would have been put in the attitude of starting out in the fight with a divided party. Secondly, by taking such a position we would have said to the whole country that we had laid down an ultimatum and order to

[23] New York *World*, September 28, 1896, as quoted in Woodward, *Watson*, 323-24. Watson shortly thereafter informed the *World's* special correspondent that, "I have been shamefully treated but I am not afraid to do my duty." He insisted that if North Carolina and Kansas had followed the Georgia precedent of refusing fusion except on Bryan and Watson electors, then Sewall would have had to withdraw. *Ibid.*

the Democrats, and that if they were not willing to accede to it, that then we were willing to see Mr. McKinley elected. Every sane man knows that the country was in no temper and would have had no patience with any party taking such a position, under the circumstances. We not only could not have gained any votes by taking such a position, but, inevitably, we would have lost them from the day such a position was taken. I admit, that if our party had been solidly united, by taking such a position we might have forced Mr. Sewall off the ticket, which would have been all right, if we could have done it; but, if he had not come off, then there is no doubting the fact that a large number of our people would have even swallowed Mr. Sewall rather than be a party, by their action, to indirectly electing Mr. McKinley." The only other possible course of action for the People's party was the one of cooperative electoral tickets, which, Butler recalled, the committee had unanimously approved. He was "more convinced to-day than when we took this position that it was the wisest and best course to pursue."

But for the sake of argument, Butler suggested that they suppose that the committee had erred at the outset of the campaign. Even if it were so, could "any man say that, at this stage of the campaign, with joint electoral tickets having been made in three-fourths of the states, and negotiations already under way in the other states, that it is wise for the committee to reverse itself, proceed to try to break up the joint electoral tickets that we have, and put out straight Bryan and Watson electoral tickets in every state?" Could Watson possibly advise such a course with the campaign over half way through? "In short," Butler plaintively requested, "tell me, if you can, what he means and what he wants?"

Butler believed that Watson was "certainly putting himself in a very false light before the country, and one that he does not deserve to be put in." Any honest political observer had to admit "that the only effect that his position can have will be to inure to the benefit of the Republican party," and "he certainly does not mean this." His position was "peculiarly unfortunate for the country as well as for our party and for himself."

Butler confessed that he had thought it barely possible that Watson had taken the peculiar course he had in an effort to win Republican support for the Populists in the Georgia state election in early October; but "upon reflection," Butler added, "I cannot conceive of him taking a position that endangers the fight all over the country, even if it would insure the success of the state ticket in Georgia."

Watson's letter to the *World* had gone out of the way to attack the Populist committee and its chairman, but Butler insisted that he was "willing to overlook all of these matters while the campaign is in progress and we are under the fire of the enemy." If Watson wanted a controversy about the wisdom of Populist strategy it would be better to have it in the newspapers after the election; but Butler, who expressed his willingness "to assume all the responsibility for the mistakes of the Committee, if it has made any," declared that he would certainly not be a party to a public controversy during the campaign. Reed should, "for Heaven's sake, see him, and try to get him to agree on some line of policy that he and the Committee can act in harmony on until the campaign is over." There would not be, must not be, war between Watson and the Populist leadership "no matter what he says or does, unless we reach the point where I believe it is absolutely necessary for the Committee to publish a statement in order to prevent the odium of helping to elect Mr. McKinley rest [*sic*] upon us."[24]

Butler sent virtually the same long letter to Watson that

24 Butler to Reed, September 29, 1896, Campaign Letterbooks, Butler MSS.

he had sent to Reed. In addition, however, Butler noted that the tone of Watson's letters indicated the Georgian wished to cut off all communication between the committee and himself. "But in spite of the tone . . .," Butler wrote, "I still hope that some common plan of action between you and the Committee can be agreed on that will be effective in unifying all voters with a common interest against McKinley and the gold standard, and thus accomplish the greatest good to our party and our country." Watson faced "a great opportunity as well as a great responsibility," for he possessed the "power to do as much, if not more, than any other man to accomplish this result." "Therefore, I appeal to you to reconsider the position that you seem to have taken."[25]

In his letters to the other members of the Populist committee Butler avowed perplexity about Watson's actions. John R. Sovereign, who was concentrating his efforts on industrial workers in the Chicago area, pointed out that "no power on earth can induce the labor organizations to make a fight on the vice presidency." He did not question Watson's honesty but observed that "as a national politician he is a failure." Butler replied: "If I did not believe that Watson was perfectly honest, I would have lost all patience with him before now, and would have gotten to a point where I would feel it was my duty to officially condemn his course. But, however much he may have angered and embarrassed me and the committee, I still have hopes of getting him to see the error of his course."

Butler believed that while the Populist headquarters were being flooded with letters protesting Watson's course, the Georgian was "receiving letters from a few impractical men, or else dishonest men, who encourage him to pursue this course; while, on the other hand, those who disapprove of his course are not writing him at all." Butler urged Sovereign

[25] Butler to Watson, September 30, 1896, *ibid.*

and others to write directly to Watson and make their views known.[26]

Butler wrote his frankest appraisals of the Watson problem to George Washburn in Chicago. While saying nothing harsh about the erratic Georgian and expressing confidence in his integrity, Butler mainly emphasized what he thought was a sadly lost opportunity. Butler alleged that at one time there might have been a chance of getting the Democrats in North Carolina to endorse Bryan-Watson electors. "But ever since Watson made his first speech in the campaign, the tide has turned against us, and the Democrats were making headway, and there was nothing left for us to do but to form a joint electoral ticket." The Populists, according to Butler, had been unable to answer the argument that no matter what they said about Sewall he at least maintained a dignified silence, not even replying to Watson's personal attacks. Now, Butler admitted, Watson's conduct lessened the chances every day for any adjustment of the Kansas situation.

One idea that Butler and Washburn had discussed was the possibility of making their demand for Sewall's withdrawal, in case of a national victory for Bryan, soon after the election. Senator Jones, Butler explained, had insisted that Sewall's withdrawal would hurt Bryan's chances "especially in those [pivotal] states where the People's party is not relatively strong, and where unreasonable prejudice even among silver men has grown up against the People's party on account of the misrepresentations of our party and principles through the partisan press." Butler had been forced to admit that there was some truth in Jones' argument, but the Populist

[26] Sovereign to Butler, September 28, 1896, Butler to Sovereign, October 1, 1896, *ibid.* To another member of the committee Butler declared that Watson was "a brilliant young man, and is as true as steel, but he is not a good politician and has not used the splendid opportunity before him to the best advantage." He was a "peculiar compound" and Butler knew of "no one that could have any influence at all with him." Butler to Dr. C. F. Taylor, September 25, October 2, 1896, *ibid.*

chairman insisted that if that were the only valid reason to be advanced for Sewall's remaining in the race, then it would not be valid as soon as the election was over, and the Populists would then officially ask for Sewall's withdrawal before the electoral college met. "He [Jones] made no promises, and entered into no agreement with reference to this matter," Butler added, "yet he was bound to admit the justness of it, and, no doubt, this is what he had in mind when he said to you that Mr. Sewall could not be withdrawn before the election."

But with Watson behaving as he was, Butler feared that the last chance of adjusting the vice-presidential situation in a manner satisfactory to the Populists was fast disappearing. If Bryan won now, the Populists would receive no credit, and if he lost, they would get the blame. And as for Washburn's statement that the Senate would probably have to elect the vice president even if Bryan won, since no vice-presidential candidate would have a majority of the electoral votes, Butler noted that according to the Twelfth Amendment the Senate would be limited to a choice between the two candidates who had received the highest number of votes, which would surely be Sewall and Hobart. "There is no possible way by which the Senate can elect Mr. Watson Vice-President," Butler concluded, "unless this matter is arranged before the electoral college meets." Clearly Watson's only hope was to go to work loyally and put victory for Bryan and national reform first and foremost.[27]

What Butler did not understand was that Watson apparently had no hope, or at least no rational and discernible one. The event that probably threw the Georgian into the final frenzy of anger and frustration was the sound thrashing that the Democrats gave the Populists, who were supported by Republicans and Prohibitionists, in Georgia's state election

[27] Butler to Washburn, October 1, 5, 6, 8, 1896, *ibid.*

on October 7, 1896. Midroad Populists had emphasized Sewall's failure to help the Democratic party carry Maine; now Watson's Populists had been whipped in Georgia, and neither of Bryan's running mates could be pictured as a decisive influence in his home state.[28]

When the Georgia Populists met their defeat, Watson, according to Reed's alarmed reports, was already so badly upset by the electoral fusion in North Carolina and Kansas that he was about ready to decline the Populist nomination. Reed had talked him out of that, but now Watson threatened serious trouble if the Populist executive committee failed to make some changes—in a hurry.[29]

Actually, though no one seems to have realized the situation at the time, Watson's power to damage Bryan's chances was rapidly diminishing. This was true not only because of the arrangement of fusion electoral tickets in the large majority of the states, including virtually all of the pivotal ones, but also because of Democratic victories in the early state elections of the deep South, where midroad sentiment was

[28] One factor in the Democratic victory in Georgia was that many Negroes supported the Democratic governor's bid for reelection because of his anti-lynching record. Although the Populists had refused formal fusion with the Republicans, many Populist leaders in the state, such as James K. Hines, made no bones about their desire for Republican support. The Republican state chairman urged Republicans to vote for the Populist candidates, and the Republicans put out no state ticket. The leading Negro newspaper in Georgia, the *Southern Age*, furnished a clue to the Negro support for the Democrats when it declared that Negroes and the *Southern Age* had supported the Populists in 1892 and 1894, yet the third party consistently refused to give Negroes any recognition. The Populists, in other words, were accused of refusing to recognize the Negro Republican voters by sharing any offices with them. "It occurs to us that if they refuse to give us recognition now when they need us most," the *Southern Age* insisted, "they will give us less when they are safely in."
This view is corroborated by the statement in the Savannah *News* that: "It is gratifying to note the movement of colored people toward the Democratic party. . . . This would seem to indicate that reasons for fear of negro domination are being rapidly dissipated." Atlanta *Constitution*, August 17, 19, September 2, 18, October 2, 1896.
[29] Reed to Butler, October 7, 9, 1896, Butler MSS.

concentrated. And despite Watson's stand, the national Populist leaders took quick and largely effective measures to close ranks during the final three weeks of the campaign.

As the political battle approached its hectic, closing weeks, however, neither the Populist nor the Democratic leaders were eager to face more trouble from Watson and his sympathizers. The race was, as far as anyone could tell, a close one. Every vote might count. Leaders in both parties began to take hurried steps to try to preserve unity among the forces allied for reform.

The Populist executive committee had earlier selected Chicago, where two of the members were already and where the others could travel with relative ease, as the place for the next meeting. Butler sent out telegrams calling the session for October 13 and urged Watson to be present. Reed replied that Watson, who had a bad throat, was under doctor's orders to remain at home for several days but could, if a meeting were really necessary, go up to Atlanta from his home in Thomson.

Since getting a quorum of the committee in the Georgia capital would be difficult if not imposible, Butler stuck by the earlier selection of Chicago. And as for the Kansas situation that loomed so large in Watson's thinking and threats, Butler frankly warned Reed, and through him Watson: "I have used all of my official power to adjust matters in Kansas, but having failed in that, I will not play the Samson and pull down the temple." If anything else were to be done, the committee would have to take the responsibility for doing it.[30]

There were two principal results of the Populist committee's meeting in Chicago: a strong and widely publicized statement reaffirming the existing policy of electoral fusion

[30] Butler to Reed, October 10, 1896, copy in Butler MSS; Butler to Breidenthal, October 10, 1896, Campaign Letterbooks, *ibid.*

and another effort to placate Watson. From the standpoint of the national presidential campaign, the statement was the most significant result. Reporters speculated prior to the meeting that the Populist leaders, together with Senator Jones and his Democratic committee, would probably act to give the Populists a part of the Kansas electors. But before the meeting Butler would only say: "We are all pulling to defeat McKinley, and while there is some friction over the division of the electors in several of the States, no action will be taken that will in the least compromise the chances of our ticket. . . . You can state authoritatively that Mr. Watson will remain on the ticket. No thought of his resignation is entertained by us." The Populist chairman, in the inevitable fashion of party chairmen, insisted that Bryan's chances were growing better daily and added, perhaps a trifle wistfully: "One of the strongest factors in the Republican campaign until recently is now one of the greatest weaknesses and that is the prodigal use of money. There is a revolt among the workingmen especially against the apparent use of money by the Republicans."[31]

The official statement that appeared in newspapers across the nation after the conference bore the marks of Butler's authorship, for the arguments were exactly the ones that he had used in his long letters of a few days earlier to Reed and Watson. The Populist committeemen first declared that they had hoped that "the patriotic action of the People's Party in National Convention in subordinating the interests of party to the success of the vital issues involved in this campaign would be met by equally unselfish devotion to a common interest on the part of the Democratic party, and that all the friends of silver could present a solid front against the

[31] St. Louis *Post-Dispatch*, October 13, 1896. Butler did admit candidly that Illinois, Kentucky, and several other sharply contested states were still doubtful.

minions of greed by supporting one ticket, the truly cooperative ticket, Bryan and Watson."

But since that hope had been disappointed, the committee
had faced the choice of supporting a straight Populist ticket
in every state or of doing everything possible "to unite the
voters of the country against McKinley and to overcome the
obstacles and embarrassments which, if the Democratic party
had put the cause first and party second, we would not have
encountered." The committee had rejected the straight
Populist ticket for every state because the party members
were "incapable of such base betrayal of their country as
would result from a division in the ranks" of reformers. The
rank-and-file Populists would have repudiated "any action on
the part of their leaders opposed to united effort at this time,
as they repudiated the old parties for treachery to their
interests."

Therefore the committee had agreed at the opening of the
campaign that division of the electors between Populists and
Democrats was the wisest course, and these joint electoral
tickets were in existence in three-fourths of the states.
Through these tickets "the People's Party will not only secure
in the Electoral College for Bryan and Watson several times
as many votes as we could have possibly secured by making a
straight fight, but we will secure the defeat of McKinley and
the gold standard, which should now be the greatest desire
of every citizen who believes in the principles of true
democracy."

Butler and his colleagues carefully refrained from naming
either Sewall or Watson, but one portion of the manifesto
was widely interpreted as a rebuke to Watson: "The danger
lies in the possibility of a certain portion of the rank and file
of the People's Party being misled by so-called leaders, who,
for reasons best known to themselves, or for want of reason,
are advising voters to rebel against the joint electoral tickets,

and put up separate electoral tickets, or to withhold their support from the joint electoral tickets."

After a warning about the Republicans' best hope being the "corrupt use of an unlimited supply of money," the Populist leaders concluded their statement with the declaration that the Populists had made "this revolution possible" and their boast would be that they were American citizens and "American citizens are more than partisans."[32]

After the conference adjourned, Butler told reporters that although the committee was still unsatisfied about the fusion arrangements in Kansas and Colorado, there was nothing to be done now that would not help McKinley. The committee members were unanimous in believing that the "address was the best thing that could be done to unite the silver forces, which is our duty above all things." "The address issued by the committee does not reflect in any way upon Mr. Watson," Butler insisted, "and it will undoubtedly be approved by him." A delegation from the committee would visit the Georgian to explain the situation to him.[33]

The Populist manifesto was cheered by ardent supporters of Bryan across the nation. Even some Democratic papers that had earlier been indifferent or scornful towards the Populists now praised the third party's role in the campaign. The St. Louis *Post-Dispatch*, for example, entitled its editorial about the address "A Patriotic Party" and declared: "In spite of friction in arranging the details of an honorable adjustment and the obtrusive self-assertion of a few men whose motives

[32] *Ibid.*, October 14, 1896. Although Edmisten of Nebraska and Dore of California did not attend the meeting, all of the other members were present and signed the statement with Butler. Butler urged Ignatius Donnelly to attend the meeting. Unable to do so because of speaking engagements, Donnelly telegraphed: "Treat Watson justly and kindly but insist Bryan must not be defeated by Populist votes." Butler to Donnelly, October 12, 1896, Donnelly to Butler, October 13, 1896, Donnelly MSS. The telegram from Butler has his name mistyped as "Maurice Mutley."

[33] St. Louis *Post-Dispatch*, October 14, 1896; Raleigh *News and Observer*, October 15, 1896.

have been open to suspicion, the Populist party has risen grandly in this campaign to the necessity of patriotic action. . . . There has been much of self-sacrifice on the part of men whose patriotism has risen superior to selfish ambition."[34]

The fusion policy which the Populists had now reaffirmed in their Chicago pronouncement gave genuine alarm to the badly frightened conservatives of the East. This fright was made clear by the widespread criticism that the Washington *Post*, an antisilver but politically independent newspaper, received when it suggested that the Democratic-Populist fusion policy gave Bryan 205 certain electoral votes. That number would put him within 19 votes of election, whereas from the still doubtful states McKinley would have to receive 84 electoral votes in order to win. To the Eastern newspapers that bitterly resented any hint of a Bryan victory, the *Post* retorted: "We cannot elect McKinley by getting together under an umbrella and resolving that Bryan is as good as defeated at the present moment. It is foolish to blind ourselves to the existence of the earnest millions who dwell beyond the Potomac and the Alleghenies. Those millions are there and they must be taken into account. We cannot dispose of them by making a great hullabaloo over here on the Atlantic coast."[35]

In Indiana, one of the most bitterly contested of the doubtful states, fusion had long been stalled. Now, just as the Populist statement appeared, the Democrats and Populists finally agreed on a cooperative electoral ticket that gave the former ten places and the latter five. The New York *Herald*,

[34] October 15, 1896. Concerning Watson, this editorial asserted that the man most highly honored by the People's party has been the "most conspicuous and persistent in thrusting his personality and his ambition between his party and its highest good," but he had lost whatever influence he might have retained when it had become known that "all his arguments against fusion, in the New York plutocratic press, have been paid for with plutocratic money at so much per article."

[35] *Post*, October 2, as quoted in Raleigh *News and Observer*, October 3, 1896.

rabid in its opposition to Bryan, reported that Hanna in Chicago was attending to Indiana where "the fusion between the popocrats and the populists on the electoral ticket has thrown most of the Hoosier Republican politicians into a panic."

From Indianapolis, the correspondent of the *Herald* reported that the Republicans had "done everything possible to stiffen the backs of the Populist leaders and prevent fusion, and are openly charged with attempts of bribery." Almost despite himself, the *Herald's* reporter paid this unwitting tribute to the allied silver parties: "The formidable showing of the Popocrats in the campaign in spite of the numerous drawbacks under which they labor is something phenomenal. Deserted by old time leaders, dismembered of their most influential followers, shorn of their sources of campaign revenue, practically without a dollar beyond what is contributed by the insulted candidates, they present a front strongly suggestive of the naked African hordes throwing themselves upon the repeating rifles and Maxim guns of civilized troops. Against them are arrayed virtually all the corporate interests of the State. The combined business interests of every city and town, with small exceptions, are hostile to them. . . . If under these circumstances they were to win this fight it would be the most remarkable campaign ever known. Such a result seems impossible."

The *Herald's* correspondent figured that despite the Democratic loss in Indiana of some 12,000 Gold Democrats, the Populists would bring about 25,000 votes to Bryan and that was close to the number of votes that the Republicans needed to put the state in the McKinley column. Indiana was said to have some 40,000 "floaters," a large percentage of whom were said to be "proverbially susceptible to financial influences." The newspaperman concluded that in Indiana "the whole thing depends upon the relative defections," and the

"Popocrats," who had "not a cent for fireworks or pictures or uniforms or other campaign tinsel," admitted "the venality of their own followers."[36]

Clearly the fusion policy created alarm in Republican circles. The Populist committee's reaffirmation of that policy gained strength from the fact that other prominent Populists who were not on the committee joined in the appeal for a united front of all reformers. Reuben F. Kolb, the veteran leader of Alabama Populists, announced as early as October 1 that since the only possible obstacle to Bryan's success in Alabama was the separate Populist electoral ticket for Bryan and Watson, he felt compelled to give his vote, and to urge other Populists to give theirs, to the Bryan-Sewall slate. Shortly after the statement from the Chicago conference, Kolb informed Butler that the midroad Populists had helped to block fusion in Alabama, although Kolb and other Populists had labored for it. Kolb believed, nevertheless, that Alabama was now safe for Bryan and that the Bryan-Sewall ticket would receive support from a majority of Populists in the state —"not because we love Watson less but Bryan more."[37]

Ignatius Donnelly, one of the best known of the northern Populists, composed an address which the Populist national committee endorsed and released on October 24. Donnelly's statement, after lavishly praising both Bryan and Watson, urged Populists not to be discouraged by the fact that Bryan had two running mates: "There will be two months between the date of the election and the day when the electors are required by law to cast their votes. Surely there is wisdom enough in the two parties which support Mr. Bryan to adjust that complication during that time and in a manner satisfactory to all."

[36] New York *Herald*, October 14, 15, 1896.
[37] Atlanta *Constitution*, October 1, 1896; Kolb to Butler, October 20, 1896, Butler MSS.

As for the integrity of the People's party, Donnelly assured his "Brethren" that the Populist organization was intact and that there was no intention "to close the academy because the first class is about to graduate with honors." Populists were merely "educating Democracy from the inside." If reformers failed in their great opportunity of 1896, they might never win, so Populists should "Forget everything else and do your whole duty."[38]

Even S. F. Norton, the Illinois Populist editor and author whom the midroaders had run against Bryan at the St. Louis convention, came out with a statement urging Populists everywhere to support Bryan. Norton argued that regardless of whether Bryan was a Populist in sentiment or not, one thing certain was "that every enemy reformers have encountered during the last twenty years we find today among Mr. Bryan's bitterest and most relentless opponents." That fact alone, according to Norton, made Bryan the friend of the Populists and his success the defeat of their enemies. Norton noted that many Populists regretted certain fusion arrangements but since no one regretted them as noticeably as did Mark Hanna, Populists had no choice but "to loyally and earnestly support Mr. Bryan—not so much for the sake of elevating him to the Presidency as for the purpose of defeating what may be appropriately and most expressively termed Mark Hanna Republicanism."[39]

With the achievement of such a large degree of unity

[38] Raleigh *News and Observer*, October 25, 1896. In requesting Donnelly to write a "bugle call" that would stir and arouse all Populists, Butler had observed: "The individual voter is governed too much, as a rule, by his local surroundings. He is apt to be guided too much by local prejudice, and fail to comprehend in a crisis like this what his full duty is, and what the responsibilities are that attach to his action or non-action." Butler to Donnelly, September 18, 1896, Campaign Letterbooks, Butler MSS.

[39] St. Louis *Post-Dispatch*, October 21, 1896. Norton sent his statement to Butler, who thanked him for the "patriotic" service and secured national distribution for it. Butler to Norton, October 22, 1896, Campaign Letterbooks, Butler MSS.

among Populists as to the necessity of supporting the fusion electoral tickets, Watson had been effectively isolated in his opposition to that policy. Nevertheless, the other result of the Populist conference at Chicago was a last effort by the national committee to soothe the Georgian who had found his role in the campaign a difficult one to fill effectively. The Populist national executive committee wrote a long private letter to Watson, explaining in candid terms how and why the committee had come to conclude that there was no alternative to the policy of the fusion electoral tickets. A subcommittee of three—Butler, Washburn, and Reed—would deliver the public address to Watson in person and "make any further explanations of the work of the campaign that may be necessary." The Populist leaders concluded their letter with an appeal for Watson's consideration and help and reminded him that they were his personal friends as well as the Populist party's official committee.[40]

Watson refused to meet the subcommittee in Atlanta but said that they could come to his home in Thomson if they wished. Although Butler returned to Washington from Chicago rather than going to Georgia as had been announced, Watson denied the newspaper reports that he had refused to see the Populist chairman. At any rate, feverish and complicated negotiations now began, and politicians, Democratic as well as Populist, descended on Thomson, Georgia.

Colonel Evan P. Howell, powerful Democrat and editor of the Atlanta *Constitution,* journeyed to confer with Watson and soon after informed him that Senator Jones found it absolutely impossible to visit Atlanta on October 19 but would send a representative. "As well as I could I outlined to him without using any names the ideas advanced by myself to you," Howell wrote, "and he telegraphed me late

[40] National Executive Committee to Watson, October 15, 1896, Thomas E. Watson MSS, Southern Historical Collection, University of North Carolina Library.

to-night his hearty concurranc [*sic*] in the idea, and stated that the member of the National Committee would be here Monday [October 19] and would be fully authorized to act in his behalf and for the committee."[41]

Reed and Washburn next spent a day at Watson's home but would only say, "We have spent a quiet day in private conversation and have greatly enjoyed this perfect October day in this genial Georgia climate." Upon their return to Atlanta, the Populist committeemen called on Howell. Clark Howell, the editor's son, attended the meeting as Senator Jones' representative; other prominent Democrats, including Patrick Walsh, who was from Augusta and one of Watson's old Democratic antagonists in Georgia's tenth congressional district, also attended the meeting. Although Washburn made some innocuous comment about a "Bryan wave" that was allegedly sweeping the country, he and Reed refused to comment on the frantic political negotiations going on in Georgia.[42]

Upon returning to Chicago, Washburn hurried to see Senator Jones with what the press association despatches referred to as an ultimatum from Watson in the form of an "alternative proposition" for submission to the Democratic campaign committee. Washburn, just prior to his conference with Jones, announced: "Mr. Watson would rather be vindicated in his own town, in his own district, in his own state and in the whole nation than be vice president. His southern pride is aroused and the people of Georgia are rallying around him because he is a Southerner. The nomination he received at St. Louis was forced upon him to unite our forces, and being at the head of a larger force than that which

[41] Howell to Watson, October 17, 1896, *ibid.* Woodward, *Watson*, 325, mentions Howell's visit and says, "Nothing came of these conferences that was announced." Woodward does state that newspaper reports had Senator Tillman visiting Thomson to promise Watson a cabinet post if he would retire from the race.

[42] Atlanta *Constitution*, October 18, 20, 1896.

elected Lincoln, he demands recognition and vindication or he will fight."

Washburn explained that there was a danger to Bryan from the disgruntled Populists who might stay at home on election day, and Watson could bring them out with a "thrilling proclamation to his party to line up" for Bryan. Watson would not accept a cabinet post, according to Washburn, and was "only anxious that his party should come out of this contest in a manner that will reflect honor on it."[43]

All of these negotiations came to naught, and the newspapers lost sight of the matter as Watson again took to the campaign trail in Alabama and Tennessee. Letters in the papers of Marion Butler, however, reveal that the subject under consideration had been a drastic plan for conciliating Watson. "I must confess that I am very much surprised at Mr. Watson's proposition to withdraw from the Vice-Presidential race to go to Congress from his district," Butler wrote Washburn. Butler thought that the switch could be arranged with the Democrats, but he feared the effect of such a move on Bryan's campaign and the Populist part in it. Did Watson think he could write an appeal to the Populists strong enough to line them up solidly for Bryan and Sewall in consideration for his being sent to Congress? "In view of his past utterances and the position which he has taken," Butler ventured, "I must say that this position of his seems to be very inconsistent, not to say absurd. I know of no man in the party who would be worth more to it in Congress than Mr. Watson, however. It is really the field where his talents peculiarly fit him for." Still, Butler advised against the plan and urged Washburn in Chicago to concentrate his efforts with Jones on an understanding about Sewall's withdrawal after the election.[44]

[43] *Ibid.*, October 21, 1896; New York *Times*, October 21, 1896.
[44] Butler to Washburn, October 24, 1896, Campaign Letterbooks, Butler MSS.

Butler's opposition to Watson's retirement from the Populist ticket together with the Democratic leaders' ultimate rejection of the scheme led to its collapse. After the election, when Watson continued his bitter attacks on Butler and his management of the campaign, Butler drafted an answer which among other things charged that Watson played the part of "knave or fool" and had done "valuable work for the gold ring for which he could have gotten good pay, though we think he did it for nothing, but from another cause." As evidence that Watson had been "simply guilty of playing the fool," Butler referred to the negotiations about the congressional seat and mentioned Watson's willingness "to sell out his party to get a two years term in Congress, with a string on the speakership."

Washburn and Reed both counseled Butler against publishing the answer to Watson, and Butler never did. Washburn expressed strong objections especially to any mention of the negotiations with Jones about a congressional seat for Watson. "That was a most sacred party secret and was urged by Watson's friends and not by himself and was simply one of the alternatives I was permitted to use with Senator Jones and is not public property," Washburn argued, "but was given to you [Butler] in confidence and should not be used under any circumstances as it would arouse much feeling."[45] Butler remained silent about the strange episode, and, as in many other aspects of the tangled events of Populist history in 1896, Watson's version of the campaign and Populist policies received most of the publicity at the time and has highly colored historical accounts as well.

Whether or not Watson himself could have been so "inconsistent" and "absurd," as Butler put it, as to have seriously considered a deal, one whereby he went to Congress

[45] Butler's unpublished answer to Watson entitled "Some Facts the Public Should Know," December, 1896, Washburn to Butler, January 13, 1897, Butler MSS.

in exchange for withdrawing as vice-presidential candidate, is debatable. The Georgian had repeatedly attacked office seekers and pictured himself as the disinterested spokesman for the agrarian masses. His followers saw Watson during the campaign of 1896 as "an uncompromising idealist." And only a day or so before Clark Howell and the other emissaries began to descend on Thomson, Watson telegraphed the Kansas midroaders that the "fusionists have abandoned principle and got into a mad scramble at the pie counter."[46]

On the other hand, Washburn did make a cryptic public statement at the time about Watson's preferring more to be "vindicated" at home than to be named vice president. And the correspondence between Washburn and Butler before and after the election was clearly not designed to raise false charges against Watson. From 1892 on Watson had tried harder to regain the tenth district congressional seat than to do anything else in his life. Although he had stubbornly contested the elections whereby his Democratic opponent repeatedly piled up allegedly fraudulent majorities in Augusta, Watson had been unable to win the prize he sought.

Perhaps Tom Watson did dream momentarily in mid-October 1896 of what seemed to be a way out of his dilemma as the Populist candidate who found himself so sadly out of step with the majority of his party and its leaders. If he did so dream perhaps the most charitable as well as most accurate thing to say about him would be what he himself later said about his condition in 1896: "Politically I was ruined. Financially I was flat on my back. How near I came to loss of mind only God who made me knows—but I was as near distraction, perhaps as any mortal could safely be. If ever a poor devil had been outlawed and vilified and persecuted and

---

[46] Woodward, *Watson*, 326; Watson's telegram in Atlanta *Constitution*, October 16, 1896. Watson and the Kansas midroaders tried to keep his name from appearing on the Populist ballot in the state, but Breidenthal took legal action that thwarted the move.

misrepresented and howled down and mobbed and threatened until he was well nigh mad, I was he."[47]

Among the Populists only the minority of midroaders would have agreed with Watson's paranoiac portrayal of persecution, but his last actions in the closing days of the campaign of 1896 did match the "distraction" that he later admitted. Even among the Georgia Populists he seemed to be losing his grip. After the Georgia Democrats again refused electoral fusion with the Populists on the basis of all thirteen electors' voting for Watson for vice president, the newspapers reported that the Populist state committee might withdraw their straight Bryan-Watson ticket in the state rather than make the weak showing that would be inevitable with four other tickets in the field—Republican, Democratic, National (Gold) Democratic, and Prohibitionist. Watson, then in Birmingham for a speech, declared: "The Georgia electors will not be withdrawn. The convention named them and they accepted the trust. They owe it to Populism in Georgia and elsewhere to stay in the field."[48]

In Alabama, where Kolb and other Populists had already rebelled against the straight Bryan-Watson ticket of the midroad Populists, Watson's continued attacks on Sewall brought cheers from the midroaders in his audiences. "When anybody says to me, 'Come down, you Southern man,' when I am asked to lie down in the dust and let this Eastern plutocrat wipe his feet on my neck," Watson declared, "would you want a Southern man to do it? (Cries of 'No!')." Reminding his listeners that they had been "wearing sackcloth and ashes long enough," Watson proclaimed that the South had been for too long "a hewer of wood" and "drawer of water" for the East and before he would betray the People's

[47] Watson in Atlanta *Journal*, August 11, 1906, as quoted in Woodward, *Watson*, 331.
[48] Atlanta *Constitution*, October 21, 22, 1896.

party, the best hope of escape from the old sectionalism, he "would die the death of a dog ten times over."[49]

While Watson proceeded to Tennessee, where electoral fusion between Populists and Democrats had also failed, the Georgia Populist committee defied Watson and withdrew the Bryan-Watson electoral ticket. As one newsman put it, this sounded the "death knell" of Georgia Populism in the national campaign. Judge Hines, the Populist gubernatorial candidate in 1894, announced that he would vote for the Democratic electors on the grounds that "because others have done wrong there's no use why Populists should do so." But other Populists announced that they would vote for McKinley rather than help Sewall become vice president. Watson virtually retired from the campaign after even his Georgia followers had disregarded his views, but he did advise one audience near his home that if they could not stomach either the Democratic or Republican electoral ticket, they could surely stay at home on election day. A solemn "Amen" from someone in the crowd greeted this pronouncement.[50]

Watson's letter accepting the Populist vice-presidential nomination provided an almost comic touch of mystery to the last two weeks of the presidential campaign. The metropolitan newspapers of the East especially exploited the matter, but all over the country people speculated about the "case of the missing letter." When he mailed the letter to

[49] *Ibid.*; New York *Times*, October 22, 1896. Watson attracted sympathy by suggesting that he was being urged to withdraw from the race, which was certainly not the case with the Populist committee and, at that late stage of the campaign, not true of Jones and the Democrats either. When told that in Alabama the electoral ticket only required a plurality to win and that there was danger of a Republican victory, Watson is quoted as having said: "Then why don't you get together—our boys are willing for it—while I am primarily opposed to fusion, I am willing to [accept] it where it will insure against McKinley electors being elected." Atlanta *Constitution*, October 23, 1896. If this was his view, it was one that he had succeeded in hiding from the public as well as from the Populist national committee.

[50] *Ibid.*, October 24, 25, 1896; Woodward, *Watson*, 327.

Chairman Butler in mid-October, Watson dropped hints about its explosive contents, and the anti-Bryan editors and newsmen began to quiver in anticipation of another sensation.

A few days later, when the Populist and Democratic representatives swarmed into Thomson, Washburn telegraphed Butler to withhold the letter from publication until further notice. Butler, who was baffled by all the furore, confessed to another member of the national committee that five days after Watson said he had mailed the letter it had not reached Washington. "I notice that Watson said in an interview one day that he had mailed it to me at Chicago, and another day that he had mailed it to me at Washington," Butler explained. "Unless it has miscarried in the mail, he certainly has not mailed it at all."[51]

The midroaders promptly added another chapter in the story of Butler's villainy and the dark conspiracy against Watson. Butler meanwhile requested Washburn to check the mail in the branch headquarters in Chicago. The Populist campaign handbook still stood in type waiting for Watson's letter, for Butler explained that he feared that on account of Watson's "sensitive disposition" he would "consider it as a reflection or slight upon him" if the book appeared without the vice-presidential candidate's letter. "I would rather publish his letter even if it is a bad document," Butler declared, "than to have the publication of the book delayed and also the suspense among our party to continue longer."[52]

Butler's own suspense ended several days before the nation's. Watson's letter had been mailed on October 14, as he claimed, and it had been postmarked as received in Washington on October 15. But it was postage due two cents.

---

[51] Butler to Dr. C. F. Taylor, October 19, 1896, Campaign Letterbooks, Butler MSS. Butler's secretary wrote Watson on the same day saying that the letter of acceptance, which the newsmen kept writing about, had not been received.

[52] Butler to Washburn, October 22, 1896, *ibid.*

Somehow in the shuffle between the postage due clerk in the Washington post office, the Senate messenger, and the Senate postmaster, the letter had lain there for over a week while the nation's curiosity built up.[53]

Contrary to what Butler had earlier said, he refused to release Watson's letter of acceptance to the public when it finally did arrive. Since the campaign would end in little more than a week, on Tuesday, November 3, Butler refused to take the responsibility for disseminating the views that Watson expressed. Watson, who had earlier not been the least bit reluctant to publicize his statements and opinions, refrained from releasing the letter himself until after the election was over.

"It is solely because of my promise to do so, that I accept the nomination," Watson began his remarkable letter. He explained that he would have preferred a straight Populist ticket at St. Louis but allowed his name to be presented for the vice-presidential place in order to harmonize the party, "it being understood that if the Populists accepted the Democratic nominee, the Democrats would accept the nominee of the Populists." Watson interpreted the fusion electoral tickets not only as a violation of the "St. Louis contract" but also as a Democratic plot to secure Populist endorsement of Sewall.

After repeating his argument about the necessity of recognizing the South, Watson charged Butler with the responsibility for the failure of the Democrats to remove Sewall from the race. No Populist could vote for Sewall without abandoning Populism, Watson argued, for "Whenever Right compromises with Wrong, it is the Right which suffers." Betray-

---

[53] Butler to Senate postmaster, October 24, 1896, J. P. Willett, the Washington postmaster, to F. H. Hoover, Butler's secretary, November 2, 1896, and J. H. Doyle, postage due clerk, to Willett, November 2, 1896, Butler MSS. Watson's letter was a long one, and his carelessness about such details as stamps and fees is illustrated by a letter from the Librarian of Congress to Watson, August 29, 1896, Watson MSS.

ing a certain immodesty as well as his ignorance of the actual sentiment among a majority of Populists, Watson declared: "I did not seek this nomination nor desire it. Had I asked the Presidential nomination of the People's Party and gone to St. Louis to claim it, no power of the Democratic emissaries could have kept it from me." He concluded by declaring that the Populist "rank and file" would never vote for Sewall electors, and if the Democratic leaders really wanted to defeat McKinley "let them lose no time in realizing this truth."[54]

Butler's reply was brief. Refusing to debate his own actions and the reasons for them, he merely pointed out that Watson was urging Populists everywhere not to support the joint electoral tickets that existed in a majority of states. "Is it possible that you fully appreciate the effect of such advice?" Butler asked. If followed, it not only would mean Bryan's defeat but would result in the Populists not receiving a single vote in the electoral college and the loss of any number of Populist congressmen and senators, not to mention state officials. Butler pointed out that in Georgia and the few other states that had followed Watson's advice the Populists would "not get a single elector, and I fear not many congressmen, if any." "Therefore, I beseech you to change at least that part of your letter that gives advice, which, if followed, would surely help the common enemy." Otherwise, Watson would have to assume the responsibility for releasing his letter.[55]

"The truth is Senator," Watson shot back, "you feel yourself to be a deeply guilty man, as indeed you are." According to Watson, the letter of acceptance had been in the Populist headquarters all along, but Butler did not dare publish it because "you felt its arraignment of you to be unanswerable." Butler had allowed his personal ill will towards him, Watson

[54] Watson to Butler, October 14, 1896, in Raleigh *Caucasian*, December 3, 1896.
[55] Butler to Watson, October 26, 1896, Butler MSS. This was also published after the election.

charged, to divert him "into a tortuous, narrow, jealous and disloyal policy which has shipwrecked the People's Party and brought the success of Mr. Bryan to a crisis of extreme peril."

After the inevitable diatribes against Sewall and the Democrats who had nominated him, Watson assailed Butler for making the fusion deals and then claiming that it was too late to apply the remedy of straight Populist tickets. Butler had not consulted, helped, or informed Watson. But the Populist committee backed Butler, the Democratic committee was against Watson—"I stand alone," the Georgian declared.[56]

Luckily for Bryan, Butler, and perhaps even for Watson, the Georgian's strange and bitter letters to the duly elected national chairman of the Populist party were kept from the public until after the election. The dominant contribution of the Populists to the last phase of the campaign was neither Watson's antics nor the speculation about his "missing" letter but the national committee's appeal from Chicago for Populist support of Bryan.

That manifesto, together with the statements from Donnelly and Norton and other Populists, more than offset in the newspapers and the public mind the erratic and perverse course of Tom Watson. Electoral fusion held in twenty-eight states, and in those most of the Populists apparently marched to the polls to vote for Bryan and reform on November 3, 1896. The Populists and their Democratic allies were not able to elect Bryan, but it was not the midroaders who caused his defeat. That was beyond the power of the Populists.

[56] Watson to Butler, October 28, 1896, Butler MSS. This is a fifteen-page, handwritten letter.

5

Defeat and Aftermath

Although the claim was small comfort in the face of McKinley's victory in the election, the national Populist leaders were able to say with truth that Bryan's defeat was not to be attributed to any failure on the part of the People's party. The leading Populist states—Texas, North Carolina, Kansas—all went for Bryan, despite the failure of Democratic-Populist electoral fusion in the first of those. In fact, Bryan carried all of the southern states except Delaware, Maryland, Kentucky, and West Virginia; and there was fusion in the last two. In all of the deep South, where the failure of fusion was the joint responsibility of both Democrats and midroad Populists, Bryan proved victorious anyhow.

West of the Mississippi Bryan won all of the electoral votes except those of California, Oregon, North Dakota, Iowa, and Minnesota; and there was electoral fusion in all five of those states. But Bryan and the cause of reform that he symbolized lost most decisively in those very states where the battle was hardest fought, in the north central states of Illinois, Indiana, Iowa, Michigan, Minnesota, and Wisconsin. Despite the fact that Democrats and Populists effected fusion in all of them and the additional fact that the number of midroad Populists in sympathy with Watson's sectional appeal was highly limited there, the Republicans won every electoral vote in those states.[1]

More or less in defiance of his own wishes, Tom Watson

received twenty-seven electoral votes for the vice presidency, five more than General Weaver had received for the presidency in 1892. Watson's largest block of votes, ironically, was the five of North Carolina's eleven that had been assigned to the Populists in the fusion arrangement in that state, and all of Watson's other votes came from states where fusion had been effected. The 217,000 or so popular votes cast for Watson electors were no proper measure of Populist voting strength, not only because of the failure of Kansas and Colorado Populists to demand places on their fusion electoral tickets but also because of Watson's and the midroad Populists' refusal to allow fusion in a number of southern states. Many Populists, in other words, voted for the Democratic electors or, as in the deep South, midroad Populists sometimes voted for McKinley or simply stayed home on election day.

Despite the "we told you so" that came from Watson and the midroad Populists after Bryan's defeat, there is little probability that their disgruntlement had anything to do with the defeat of the national reform movement.[2] The real question about the outcome of the election is this: why was Bryan unable to win any of the north central states? With their relatively large number of electoral votes, the addition

[1] The most convenient summary of the election results is to be found in *Appleton's Annual Cyclopaedia*, 1896 (New York, 1897), 673, 770. McKinley received 271 electoral votes to 176 for Bryan; in the popular vote the former received over 7,000,000 votes and the latter about 6,500,000.

[2] In California the straight People's party electoral ticket polled 22,234 votes but the Republican lead over the Democratic-Populist fusion ticket was 23,613. In Kentucky, the Republicans won by a scant 277 votes; there was no separate Populist electoral ticket and the 5,084 votes for Palmer on the National (Gold) Democratic ticket obviously hurt Bryan there much more than any midroad Populist disaffection. Given California's nine and Kentucky's eleven electoral votes, however, plus the narrowness of the Republican victory in those states, those were the two states where midroad Populist sentiment could have been important. In Kansas and Texas, both of which voted for Bryan, midroaders polled, respectively, 1,240 and 77,985 votes. Edgar E. Robinson, *The Presidential Vote, 1896-1932* (Stanford University, California, 1934), *passim*.

of them—Illinois, Indiana, Iowa, Michigan, Minnesota, and Wisconsin—plus either Kentucky or California to the Bryan column would have meant a victory for reform in 1896.

Marion Butler, the Populist chairman, and his committee, no less than the leaders of the two major parties, fully appreciated the strategic role of the north central states from the outset of the campaign. Despite the fact that Populism's center of gravity, as determined by actual voting strength and membership, was in other sections of the country, the Populists opened branch headquarters for the campaign in Chicago and worked assiduously to help win support for the fusion electoral ticket in the surrounding states.

These were the states that clearly did not fit into the simple pattern of an alliance of South and West that some agrarians liked to talk about in 1896. The Democratic national convention itself in its initial preference for a vice-presidential nominee from the East and Bryan in his warm and courteous treatment of Sewall throughout the campaign displayed sensitivity to the sectional issue and a desire to escape the charge of ignoring the most populous part of the country. Most of the national Populist leaders likewise saw that a too simple geographical or sectional approach hurt more than it helped in the most crucial states, and they accordingly emphasized an economic and class analysis of the campaign issues.

Tom Watson, on the other hand, never seemed to discern the limitations of his sectional appeal as far as the states of the old Northwest were concerned. He occasionally mentioned the importance of Illinois or Indiana or one of the other states in his correspondence, but the approach more typical of him was illustrated by this declaration to an audience at Stone Mountain, Georgia, shortly before the state election: "I thought from the first that this campaign should be made on sectional lines—the south and west against the

north and east. That is the real issue, and why not be honest
and say so? Our interests are opposed to those of the east."[3]

A Republican wag quipped during the campaign that
Bryan had "two vices to McKinley's one," and all enjoyed
the joke. Bryan himself could hardly be said to have enjoyed
the fact of the two running mates during the campaign,
especially with the midroad Populists screaming as they did.
But he reconciled himself to the anomaly and apparently
opposed the idea of Watson's withdrawing from the race in
mid-October just as he had stood staunchly by Sewall during
the Populist convention in St. Louis. Composing his still
useful memoir of the campaign immediately after its termina-
tion, Bryan announced his own conclusion about the matter:
"Looking back over the campaign I am now convinced that
under the conditions then existing two Vice-Presidential
candidates were better than one, and that, notwithstanding
the embarrassment at the time, the silver cause made a
better showing than it would have done if Mr. Sewall had
withdrawn in favor of Mr. Watson, or Mr. Watson in favor
of Mr. Sewall."[4]

Bryan's point may be conceded, but the fact remains that
he was not strong enough to win in the north central states.
Economically those states had long been drawing closer to
the East, and with reference to the Civil War the dominant
sentiment in them was certainly northern and Republican.
The presence on the Democratic ticket of a New England
businessman did not prevent some Republicans from harking
back to the "bloody shirt," the venerable type of sectionalism
that had proved so useful to Republicans since 1865. One
innovation in the pattern in 1896 was that the Gold Democrats too were not above resorting to the charge of neo-

[3] Atlanta *Constitution*, October 2, 1896.
[4] Bryan, *First Battle*, 298; the earlier quip is from Wayne C. Williams,
William Jennings Bryan (New York, 1936), 173.

Confederate aggression. J. Sterling Morton, for example, Cleveland's secretary of agriculture from Nebraska and a rabid foe of financial reform, declared that in "the Southern Confederacy the same leaders who are in command of the picket guards for free silver at 16 to 1 were leading financiers [in the war]." Morton charged that the "Confederate Generals now in command of the Bryan campaign seem to desire to accomplish, by false finance, that which they failed to bring about by arms, national dishonor and disgrace."[5]

Although McKinley himself carefully eschewed appeals to the "bloody shirt" in his front-porch speeches, lesser Republicans and other Gold Democrats besides Morton joined in the tried-and-true chorus that had for so long made reform impossible and furnished protection for economic conservatism. Even the New York *Times*, which criticized the Republican party's past record with reference to the South, warned that for "the old Confederate States to be massed together in a solid support of Bryan and the policy of disaster and dishonor which he stands for would make a very bad impression." Such a southern voting pattern, according to the *Times*, would "be evidence of a certain lack of patriotism and of loyalty to our institutions, and will be damaging to that confidence which has been slowly growing between the people of the North and South."

When various "goldbugs" attacked the Bryanites for being in league with former slaveholders and plotting "another scheme of secession more treasonable than the first," the St. Louis *Post-Dispatch* pointed out that the "effort to 'fire the

---

[5] Raleigh *News and Observer*, October 16, 1896. One of the Southerners whom Morton had named in his attack, Senator John T. Morgan of Alabama, replied: "I have never thrown any stones at that barn rat, and I do not see why he should refer to me by name as a rebel. I am not aware that in the army I had to fight any member of this administration. I may have had to fight Mr. Cleveland's substitute, and I have long since forgiven the substitute, because he was man enough to fight." *Ibid.*, October 17, 1896.

Northern heart' has the very obvious purpose of changing the subject." The St. Louis paper insisted that because southerners chose to "align themselves with Illinois, Indiana, Iowa, and Kansas rather than with Wall Street" they had again to face the old charges of disloyalty, but the "attempt to revive the old sectionalism is mere Wall Street imbecility."[6]

Whether an imbecility or not, the Republican and Gold Democratic appeal to the old sectionalism was merely one factor that hurt Bryan in the north central states. Probably much more important in explaining the reformers' loss of those states was their apparent inability to win massive support from the industrial workers who already crowded Chicago, Indianapolis, and the other cities of the region.

Failure to win the workers' votes was not due to any lack of effort on the part of the Populists. One of the reformers' most widely circulated documents was a petition for bimetallism which the heads of the various labor organizations had signed and presented to Congress in 1895. Demanding an "immediate return to the money of the Constitution as established by our fathers, by restoring the free and unlimited coinage of both gold and silver at the present ratio of 16 to 1," these allied leaders of farmers and industrial workers foreshadowed the political alliance of the campaign of 1896. Some of the signers and their organizations were: J. R. Sovereign, Grand Master Workman of the Knights of Labor; Samuel Gompers, President of the American Federation of Labor; Marion Butler, President of the National Farmers' Alliance and Industrial Union; H. H. Trenor, President of

---

[6] New York *Times*, October 31, 1896; St. Louis *Post-Dispatch*, September 18, 1896. Ignatius Donnelly asserted that the popular prejudice against the Democratic party caused Bryan to lose Minnesota. "The Republican speakers claim[ed] that the Peoples' Party men have all turned Democrats, and then they raked over the Democracy during the War, and drove our Republican friends back to their 'first love.'" Donnelly to W. A. Bentley, December 29, 1896, Donnelly MSS.

the United Brotherhood of Carpenters and Joiners; P. M.
Arthur, Grand Chief of the United Brotherhood of Loco-
motive Engineers; C. A. Robinson, President of the Farmers'
Mutual Benefit Association; Frank P. Sargent, Grand Master
of the Brotherhood of Locomotive Firemen; and John Mc-
Bride, President of the United Mine Workers.[7]

In addition to the silver issue on which the organized
farmers and workers had agreed long before the campaign,
both Democrats and Populists included other planks in their
platforms that were especially designed to appeal to the
workers. The Democratic platform echoed one of the strongest demands of the labor groups in calling for the protection
of American labor by the prevention of the "importation of
foreign pauper labor to compete with it in the home market."
The Populist platform called for a program of public works
to relieve the unemployed during industrial depressions. Both
parties endorsed the income tax and condemned "government
by injunction" as it had been most conspicuously displayed
in the Pullman strike of 1894 and the subsequent arrest,
conviction, and imprisonment of Eugene Debs.

To capitalize on these obvious bids for labor support, the
Populist national executive committee assigned one of its
members, John R. Sovereign of the Knights of Labor, to the
Populists' branch headquarters in Chicago and gave him the
special assignment of organizing the campaign among the
industrial workers. Marion Butler too, despite his wholly
agrarian background, revealed a clear awareness of the crucial
nature of the workers' votes. When certain railroad companies distributed an antisilver circular among their employees, Butler prepared and had printed an answer. "If this
is not the correct answer," he declared to Senator Jones,

7 Bryan, *First Battle*, 166-67. For evidence of this petition during the
campaign and its cheering effect on Bryan's agrarian backers, see the Raleigh
News and Observer, October 4, 1896.

"then we must have one. The only hope of the gold men now is to array the wage earner against the farmer, and we must meet it."[8]

To Debs, who strongly supported Bryan and who consequently had refused to allow Henry Demarest Lloyd to nominate him at the Populist convention in St. Louis, Butler also sent a copy of his answer to the railroad companies' antisilver appeal. Requesting Debs to publish the Populist answer in the newspaper of his American Railway Union, Butler also took the occasion to explain the part he had played in the Senate in attempting to pass legislation that would prevent such injustices in the future as Debs had allegedly suffered at the hands of the federal courts.[9]

John McBride, head of the United Mine Workers and former president of the American Federation of Labor, declared that "not one single bona fide labor paper in the United States" was supporting McKinley and that every labor organization of any consequence had declared for silver and against government by injunction. "When the moneyed men of the land all rush to the support of McKinley and the gold standard," McBride insisted, "it is time for the labor leaders to get on the other side, because experience has demonstrated that there is nothing in common between the men who make wealth and the men who take wealth."[10]

The loyal support of Bryan from Debs, McBride, Gompers, and other leaders of organized workers was clear enough, but

[8] Butler to Jones, September 7, 1896, Campaign Letterbooks, Butler MSS.
[9] Butler to Debs, September 12, 1896, Butler to the *Legal Adviser*, Chicago, September 7, 1896, *ibid.*
[10] Raleigh *News and Observer*, September 6, 1896. McBride was attacking the views of Terence V. Powderly, former head of the Knights of Labor, who was one of the few labor leaders who campaigned for McKinley. Even the Republicans admitted that organized labor was against them. One of them wrote from Chicago: "The labor organizations are against us to a man. Impossible to teach them. They are more interested in the question of Federal jurisdiction over strikes than the money question." New York *World*, September 12, 1896, as quoted in Josephson, *The Politicos*, 691.

the important question was about the views of the vast majority of the workers who were still unorganized. Henry George, famed author of *Progress and Poverty*, was in many ways the pioneer and giant among the reformers of the Gilded Age. Not only did he declare his enthusiastic adherence to the silver cause, but he also traveled around to various industrial centers during the campaign to write firsthand accounts for the New York *Journal*.

In Chicago George found that the leaders in the Bryan campaign were confident about support from organized labor but doubtful about the unorganized majority of workers, and he was especially interested in ascertaining if the same pattern held in Cleveland. As well as he could determine, George reported, pro-Bryan sentiment among the organized laborers was, if anything, even stronger in the Cleveland area than in Chicago. The National Plasterers' Association had held its annual meeting in the Ohio city a week earlier and the National Carpenters' Association met while George was there; the support for Bryan in both groups seemed to be strong and general. George also found that the workers in the Cleveland area felt some bitterness and suspicion about labor trouble in a local plant where, the workers believed, the company was determined to break the union. "There is an idea among the men that if McKinley wins this effort will be generally made," he added.

In one of the public squares of Cleveland, Henry George found another colorful facet of the campaign. Bryan had spoken there almost a month earlier, and "from that day to the present moment, a sort of perpetual discussion has gone on in this public square." The men who formed the changing audience, many or most of whom were unemployed, insisted on certain proprieties and on each side's having a fair hearing. The more or less permanent chairman who presided over the openair meetings was "a round, full-built man, named Orr,

who was a foreman of dock ore handlers in the employ of
Mark Hanna until he attended the St. Louis Populist convention as a delegate" and was discharged upon his return.
Mark Hanna's agents would have been smart to retain the
man, George asserted, for he devoted "his enforced leisure
to the most effective work toward defeating McKinley, by
acting as a sort of common consent chairman for this common
people's perpetual parliament." All the information that
George could get suggested that the unemployed men were
nearly unanimous for Bryan.[11]

Intrigued by the widely publicized accounts of the large
delegations of workers who visited McKinley's home, Henry
George went to Canton, Ohio, then the Republican Mecca,
to see for himself. He joined a delegation that had been
brought in on a special train from a "tin plate mill" and
marched up to the front yard of McKinley's residence. "Governor McKinley is a very careful man in such matters,"
George found. "The speaker who is to make the address [for
the visiting delegation] is first called in, and if a copy has not
been furnished in advance, the candidate learns what is to be
said by him, in order to provide against such disaster as befell
Blaine at the hands of Rev. Dr. ["Rum, Romanism, and
Rebellion"] Burchard. He then comes out, listens to the
address and reads his reply, which is afterwards revised before
being sent to the press." George concluded, after this carefully staged affair, that he had rather "travel around like

[11] Henry George to New York *Journal*, as quoted in Raleigh *News and
Observer*, September 23, 25, 1896. When a government official suggested
that Bryan's unprecedented speechmaking tours were undignified and would
cause him to be beaten badly, George asked Governor Altgeld his view
and reported that the Illinois governor thought that: "Bryan was doing more
for the success of his party than any other hundred of the ablest speakers
could possibly do, and that the effect on the people of seeing and hearing
the man they were asked to vote for, and even where it was impossible for
them to do that, of knowing that he was doing his utmost to get among
them, and talk to them face to face, was counting for more than an elaborate organization and an army of the best speakers." *Ibid.*

Bryan, hard as that must be, than stay in one place and make speech after speech, especially if I felt it necessary to write and revise them."[12]

After talking with his own acquaintances in Canton and with silverites who gathered around the local courthouse, George believed that there was "the same coercion and the same reaction from it, and the same word goes about among workingmen to wear [McKinley] buttons or join clubs, or to 'spoil the Egyptians' by taking anything that is offered from the Hanna funds, but to express their real opinions at the polls." The Bryan workers in Canton were even optimistic about their chances for carrying the county; Populists and Democrats were cooperating, and the Populists were "working in their own way like beavers."

As for himself, Henry George declared on the eve of the election and after completing his tour that he would vote for Bryan "with firmer confidence and a clearer conviction of duty" than he had felt since his first vote was cast for Abraham Lincoln. "In form the struggle is on the currency question," Henry George wrote. "But these are only symbols, and behind them are gathered the world-opposing forces of aristocratic special privilege and democratic freedom. I can have no question of how I ought to vote."[13]

Another account of a workers' delegation at Canton, writ-

[12] *Ibid.*, September 28, 1896. Mrs. Mary E. Lease, the well-known Kansas Populist, obtained an interview with McKinley. She reported, no doubt with gleeful malice, that after desultory conversation about how weary McKinley was from all the visitors, she threw out a reference to "the octopus of mortgaged indebtedness." "A startled look, half fear, lest he had given utterance to an unguarded statement, leaped into Major McKinley's eyes," Mrs. Lease declared. Every effort to renew the conversation failed, and she concluded that, if a man could not act unless he first had knowledge, "then action cannot be expected from Major McKinley, for apparently he is not in possession of any knowledge." With his apparent lack of self-confidence, he impressed the female Populist as little more than "a mile-stone having engraved upon it the distance more or less from the National capitol." *Ibid.*, October 18, 1896.

[13] *Ibid.*, September 28, 1896; St. Louis, *Post-Dispatch*, November 8, 1896.

ten from a perspective quite different from that of Henry George and by a reporter who apparently was unconscious of the ironies involved, suggests some of the obstacles that the reformers faced among the unorganized workers in 1896. Three special trains delivered 2,500 "brawny workingmen" from Homestead, Pennsylvania, which had earlier been the scene of one of the bitterest and bloodiest lockouts of the era. Marching up the streets "with military precision behind its own squad of Homestead policemen," the delegation was said to have made an imposing sight. After the "Homestead Glee Club sang lustily and tunefully several campaign songs," the superintendent of the transportation department at Andrew Carnegie's vast plant spoke first: "We are of the Homestead Steel Works, which employs over 5,000 men and turns out 90,000 tons of finished material per month and under the McKinley [tariff] law we could double that. It is too bad to see such men and such a plant lie idle, all caused by a lot of theorists. They surely do not expect to get something for nothing, or change the law of supply and demand; nor yet do they expect that Coxey and his hoboes will ever be made rich by an act of Congress. We are perfectly satisfied with the Republican platform and with you for our leader, and when you are elected, which you will be as surely as the sun shines, enact a tariff law that shall give us protection from the pauper labor of Europe, and pass a law declaring gold the standard money of the country, and the women and children who are now living on black coffee and bread, will say, 'God bless you, McKinley, and long may you live to bless mankind.' "

After mounting a chair to respond and being greeted with a "tumultous outburst" by these happy, unorganized steelworkers, McKinley began: "The Republican party has always believed in 'Homesteads.' (Laughter and applause.) Whether it be the homesteads upon the public domain in the far West or whether it be homesteads in the busy centres of manufacturing industries. . . . If there is one day's labor for sixteen workingmen, you would not get as good wages as though there were sixteen days' work for one workingman. (Laughter and applause.) And that is the sort of 16 to 1 we want in the United States." Then as the delegation from Homestead left, "music of advancing bands announced the approach of a thousand employees from the office of the Pennsylvania Railway in Pittsburgh" and 700 workingmen from McKeesport, Pennsylvania.[14]

If industrial workers had been subjected only to railway excursions to Canton and McKinley's carefully censored platitudes, no Bryanite could have fairly complained. But the intensity of feeling about the issues involved in the campaign of 1896 led to a pattern of intimidation, some of it subtle and some brutally overt, that effectively robbed an incalculable number of citizens of their freedom of choice. This quickly becomes apparent to any one who spends some time with the newspapers of the period. There was no employers' conspiracy. Mark Hanna did not exercise vast and mysterious power to control factory owners scattered across the nation. Such measures were not necessary when the battle lines were as clearly drawn as they seemed to most Americans to be in 1896. To catalog all of the instances of the intimidation of workers would be as tiresome as it would be impossible, but perhaps a few examples may serve to suggest the situation that existed.

That a major depression had prostrated the economy was true enough. But a bad situation seemed to get drastically worse in the summer of the great campaign. The New York *Times,* then certainly no purveyor of stories slanted to arouse sympathy for underlings, reported that the last shaft of the

[14] New York *Times,* September 13, 1896. When the Populist committee could not find funds to send out speakers, it is noteworthy that the Republicans could pay for large audiences to visit McKinley.

Rockefeller iron mines in Bessemer, Michigan, had been closed down, leaving fewer than 1,000 men with jobs out of the 8,000 who had once been employed there. The president of the company explained that, "Our regular customers have not bought their supply, and they tell us that they find it impossible to sell their pig-iron product because the agitation in favor of free silver has stopped investments in enterprises which would otherwise have enabled them to operate their works as usual."[15]

In St. Louis, Missouri, an iron works that employed about 700 men closed its door on August 1, and the president informed a newsman that he attributed the decline in orders "to the free silver agitation, and to the [Democrats'] Chicago platform." The reporter discovered that shortly before the mills were closed each worker had been given a copy of an antisilver speech, "How Free Coinage Will Affect the Workingman," by John G. Carlisle, President Cleveland's secretary of the treasury. At the end of August another factory in St. Louis that employed about 170 men closed down until after the election. On the night that it closed the vice president in charge of the factory's operation informed the Eighth Ward Republican Club that the agitation for free silver had led to the cessation of work and that he had made an "exhaustive explanation" of the evils of free silver to all the employees before discharging them.[16]

Although supporters of reform from Bryan and Senators Jones and Butler down to the humblest Democrat or Populist vigorously protested these widely repeated incidents, redress of the workers' grievances was rare. One blatant case, however, presented the rare spectacle of an overbearing employer

[15] New York *Times*, August 4, 1896.
[16] St. Louis *Post-Dispatch*, August 2, September 1, 1896. These stories were not written in the sensational, biased manner that characterized much of the journalism of the time but were calm and factual.

who had to back down in the face of public pressure. The owner of a department store in St. Louis discharged a dozen of his employees, including a department head or two, allegedly because they were advocates of free silver and therefore "anarchists" and unfit to work in the store. When the St. Louis *Post-Dispatch* published the story along with affidavits from the discharged employees and the Democratic state committee threatened legal action, the employer hastily bowed before a part of the public's anger. He reinstated the twelve employees and took half-page advertisements to announce that the company had never paid any attention to the "Religious Belief, Politics or Nationality" of any person seeking employment there. Furthermore: "Our store will be closed on Election Day, Tuesday, Nov. 3d, at 1 P. M., so that all our employees will have ample time to VOTE AS THEY PLEASE."[17]

Unfortunately for the reform parties, factories, mines, and railways were not so susceptible to the outraged opinion of a part of the public as a locally owned department store was. Consequently, the number of closed mills, discharged workers, and orders placed on condition of Bryan's defeat increased as the campaign continued. The New York *Times* noted that in addition to hundreds of orders conditioned on McKinley's election at the iron and steel mills in Pennsylvania, there was a long published list of proposed issues of municipal bonds which had been deferred until after the election. In most of the cases the money was needed to construct public works. The election of Bryan would deprive laborers of the much-needed employment but "the election of McKinley will give it to them with very little delay."

[17] *Ibid.*, October 11, 12, 13, 1896. The *Post-Dispatch* on October 16 reported that the *World* was the only newspaper in New York to mention the incident at the St. Louis department store—but the *World* had it that the discharged workers were for McKinley and that this was a "case of flagrant intimidation on the part of a free silver enthusiast."

As opposed to Bryan as the *Times* was, even it speculated editorially that businessmen might be "aggravating a state of mind that is unhealthy in itself, and that will, after the election, produce a reaction that may easily be mischievous." While nineteen out of twenty businessmen were confident of Bryan's defeat, they were "waiting and hesitating, 'taking in sail' for possible stormy weather, or, at best, not letting out any." The *Times* considered the business world's "curious state of mind" as "a striking commentary on the character of Bryan and his party and their policy." The Nebraskan possessed the "belief of an ignorant fanatic in the doctrine he represented" and was, moreover, "a demagogue and a revolutionist by nature without any anchorage of knowledge, or experience, or sober purpose to steady him." The New York newspaper concluded that his election would not be a fatal disaster to the nation but "it would be terrible." Still, businessmen for their own good as well as the country's might "wisely act with more courage and decision."[18]

Given the defenselessness of the vast majority of unorganized industrial workers, there is nothing surprising in the fact that Bryan was unable even to carry the larger cities of the Midwest, much less to pile up the large majorities there that helped elect Democratic presidential candidates after

---

[18] New York *Times*, October 21, 22, 1896. The businessmen's confidence apparently returned with something of a rush after McKinley's victory. The "world's largest" refrigerator company in Michigan announced that it would resume work after being closed all summer and would reemploy from 300 to 450 men. There was an order for 3,000 ice-boxes that had been conditioned on Republican victory. Silk mills in Hartford, Connecticut, were resuming full-time operation after running on short time for several months, and manufacturers in the area reported an "improved feeling in business" and confidence that as surely as it had been promised an era of prosperity was at hand. A textile mill in New York state resumed full operation with a single order that had been placed conditionally for "5,000 pairs of pants," and in Terre Haute, Indiana, two rolling mills hired 400 more men than had been used during the summer. Atlanta *Constitution*, November 9, 1896. These are only a few of the instances of renewed business activity reported in one day's issue of the Atlanta newspaper.

1932.[19] Leaders who were sympathetic with labor hinted during the campaign that the unorganized workers constituted a highly vulnerable portion of the farmer-labor phalanx that was the hope of reformers in 1896. Eugene Debs, for example, declared early in the campaign that if the election were held then, Bryan would carry even the eastern states with the exception of Pennsylvania. "In Pennsylvania labor is more completely subjugated than in any other State of the Union, and corporate influences better organized," Debs explained. "The miners are largely Italians, Hungarians, and Poles, who have displaced American labor and they do not hesitate to vote according to the orders they receive." An Iowan Populist declared it was "a great fight" with silver "a mere bauble compared with the real bottom struggle now going on for human rights." But the outcome depended on the labor vote. "Will they have sense enough to see beyond a day's work?" the Iowan asked. "I think the plutes fear defeat and are playing a desperate game and risking all." Florence Kelley in Chicago feared that wholesale coercion in Chicago and elsewhere meant that Altgeld and Bryan would lose the state. "There may be more moral courage among the wage earners than I'm calculating upon," Miss Kelley realistically admitted. "But I see no reason for expecting much."[20]

[19] William Diamond, "Urban and Rural Voting in 1896," *American Historical Review*, XLVI (January 1941), 289-90, shows that in the east north central section—Wisconsin, Michigan, Illinois, Indiana, and Ohio—neither the cities nor the rural areas gave majorities to Bryan and there was, in general, little of the tension between urban and rural voting that Diamond found in most other sections in varying degrees. In the west north central section—Minnesota, Iowa, Kansas, Nebraska, and Missouri—Bryan carried the last three states but lost the cities in all.

[20] St. Louis *Post-Dispatch*, August 8, 1896; A. W. C. Weeks to Lemuel H. Weller, October 22, 1896, Weller MSS, Wisconsin State Historical Society; Florence Kelley to Henry D. Lloyd, October 15, 1896, Lloyd MSS. Pollack, *Populist Response to Industrialism*, 61-63, suggests, correctly in this writer's opinion, that the reason for the failure of the farmer-labor coalition

Just as Populist and Democratic efforts to win support from the urban workers in the pivotal states apparently failed with the unorganized majority, Bryan and his associates in the campaign were likewise unsuccessful in persuading the majority of the rural farm population in those states to vote for reform. Not only were farmers in Iowa, Wisconsin, Minnesota, and Michigan traditionally Republican from the Civil War on, but historians agree that agriculture in the north central states never suffered as cruelly as it had in the drought-stricken regions farther west and in the South. As one historian has put it, "Bryan failed to carry the farmers with him where he needed them the most, in the Old Northwest and upper Mississippi Valley."[21]

Despite their traditional Republicanism, farmers in the pivotal states did suffer in the major depression that began in 1893. Plummeting farm prices coupled with other grievances shared with agrarians in other regions created unrest, and the Republican campaign leaders in 1896 concentrated on soothing the uneasiness of the farmers in the crucial states no less than the Populists and Democrats tried to capitalize on it. Professor Gilbert Fite has shown how the Republicans flooded the section with campaign material arguing the thesis that low farm prices had nothing to do with the gold standard but derived solely from domestic overproduction and foreign competition. The Republicans furnished no inkling as to how supply and demand might be brought into balance

---

in 1896 lay with labor and that historians have erred in regarding the agrarians as the stumbling block. Samuel P. Hays, *The Response to Industrialism, 1885-1914* (Chicago, 1957), 66, states that the largest of the labor organizations, the American Federation of Labor, had only 278,000 members in 1898.

[21] Gilbert C. Fite, "Republican Strategy and the Farm Vote in the Presidential Campaign of 1896," *American Historical Review*, LXV (July 1960), 804-805. Professor Fite notes that Minnesota, Iowa, and Ohio had voted Republican in every presidential election between the Civil War and 1896 and Illinois and Wisconsin had voted Democratic only in 1892.

other than through the general prosperity that they promised
with the return to the higher protective tariff which they
perennially stood for. But their headquarters in Chicago,
"the real centre of the educational part of the campaign"
according to Mark Hanna's biographer, lavishly dispensed
pamphlets and materials especially prepared for distribution
to the rural weekly newspapers and farm journals and all
stressing the theme of overproduction.[22]

Farmers who could not be persuaded that overproduction
and President Cleveland's trifling reductions in the tariff
rates were the sources of agricultural depression might have
been influenced in other ways. Farmers obviously could not
be discharged or even intimidated about their political views
in the way that industrial workers were. But the enemies of
silver had other approaches that could be used in the hinter-
lands. A reporter for a British journal found that eastern
insurance companies that owned mortgages on farms in Iowa,
Indiana, Illinois, and surrounding states sent their numerous
agents into the presidential campaign in October. The companies, "fearing things were running in favor of Bryan, sent
these agents to see personally every farmer and come to an
understanding that if McKinley were elected they would
grant five years' extension of the loan at a low rate of
interest."[23]

[22] *Ibid.*, 794-98. With regard to the political effect of the rise in wheat
prices just prior to the election, Fite admits that the times were not actually
improving for farmers late in 1896 but suggests, quite correctly, that many
midwestern farmers may have thought they were. "Voters do not necessarily
act on what is true, but on what they think is true. The possibility should
not be overlooked that the widespread and intense prosperity-is-coming campaign may have won a sizable number of farm voters, many of whom were
traditionally Republican anyway, but who had temporarily deserted the party
in protest against low prices and hard times." *Ibid.*, 801. Hanna's superb
organizational work is described in Herbert Croly, *Marcus Alonzo Hanna:
His Life and Work* (New York, 1912), 209 ff.

[23] *St. James Gazette*, November 6, 1896, as quoted in Josephson, *The
Politicos*, 702. North Carolinians, and probably others, received notices from
their insurance companies that the free coinage of silver would result in

And for those farmers, and workers too for that matter, who displayed a stubborn interest in the possibility of relief from the grinding deflation through the free coinage of silver, the Republicans also had an answer. Its logic may have clashed with that of the theme of overproduction, but American politicians of whatever party have seldom paid much attention to logic. Not only did the Republican platform promise an effort for silver through "an international agreement with the leading commercial nations of the earth," but McKinley himself had a strongly prosilver record during his earlier incarnation as a congressman from Ohio. "I have always been in favor of the free and unlimited coinage of the silver product of the United States, and have so voted on at least two occasions during the time I have been in public life," he had declared in 1890. "With me political and economic questions are a conviction."[24]

Early in 1896, months before the conventions and campaign, a Republican senator had frankly asserted that to secure an international agreement for silver would be just as impossible "either now or hereafter, as to secure a railroad connection between here and the planet Mars." Conservative eastern newspapers like the New York *Evening Post*, which frankly adhered to the gold standard, assailed the talk of international bimetallism as "solemn fooling, if not worse." Another spoke of "chasing a moonbeam" which fed among the unemployed and the chronically poor "a restless fever, which is death to genuine prosperity." Democratic and Populist editors and political leaders were, for once, quite in agreement with the candid advocates of monometallism about the essential unreality of any international agreement.

---

policies being paid in dollars worth only fifty cents. Raleigh *Caucasian*, August 13, 1896.

[24] Congressman Wm. McKinley, Jr., to E. S. Perkins, September 27, 1890, as quoted in New York *Times*, September 30, 1896.

England's attachment to the gold standard was too unshak-
able. But that did not prevent Mark Hanna and the Republican headquarters in Chicago from utilizing the idea of an
international agreement to the fullest, wherever and whenever it was needed.[25]

"The free-silver disease is yielding to treatment . . . ,"
Hanna announced in New York at one point during the
campaign. "A great deal more work is being done [in the
Midwest] than in the Eastern States." Another and more
famous remark of Hanna's was, "He [Bryan] is talking silver
all the time, and that's where we've got him."[26] These
remarks of the Republican generalissimo of 1896 have often
been interpreted as evidence of Bryan's mistake in emphasizing silver, the issue that all the reform parties had agreed to
push to the forefront.

Another and more likely interpretation is that Hanna and
Republican campaigners treated the "free-silver disease" in
the Midwest as in the South not by talk of the gold standard
but by pushing forward the idea of an international agreement
as the safest and surest route to bimetallism. The Republicans, in other words, could "get" Bryan for "talking silver
all the time" because they could "talk silver" too. The lines
were drawn more clearly and the issues posed more honestly
in 1896 than in any campaign in many decades. But the
Republican party's promise of an effort for an international
agreement on silver, no matter how unrealistic the promise,
furnished the precise and critical ambiguity that may have
been one of the decisive factors in McKinley's victory in the
north central states.[27]

[25] New York *Evening Post* and other Republican newspapers as quoted in
Raleigh *News and Observer*, October 3, December 25, 1896.
[26] New York *Times*, September 24, 1896; the second quotation is given,
among other places, in Faulkner, *Politics, Reform, and Expansion*, 206.
[27] After the election the New York *Evening Post* deplored Hanna's statement that "farmers and laborers in the western cities were won over to the
support of McKinley by explaining to them that we stood on the St. Louis

There is evidence, finally, that some shrewd observers at the time understood why Bryan had lost the election. Marion Butler explained to a prominent Populist in Kentucky that the "great northwestern states" had to be captured before the fight for reform could be won; they had been lost in 1896 when the Republicans succeeded in winning too much of the farmer-labor vote. Josephus Daniels, visiting Washington not long after the election, talked with Senator Jones and with other prosilver leaders. The Tarheel editor found that Jones and his allies "got exactly what they expected from the East —nothing." They knew too that they "lost in the central West in the great cities, and in the disinclination of Republican farmers to break away from their party in view of McKinley's votes in Congress for silver."[28]

In addition to the above reasons for Bryan's failure in the pivotal states, the role of the churches, both Protestant and Roman Catholic, is an imponderable factor that should be at least mentioned. Professor Richard Hofstadter in his devastating essay on "Bryan: the Democrat as Revivalist" manages to convey the impression that the Nebraskan was uniquely naive and simple minded in thinking that morality had much to do with the issues in 1896. Declaring that the "Great Commoner was a circuit-riding evangelist in politics" and always a "provincial politician" who followed "a provincial populace in provincial prejudices," Hofstadter argues that Bryan premised his whole political career on the belief that "social problems are essentially moral—that is to say, religious." And from 1896 to the Scopes trial and his death, Bryan "was

---

[Republican] platform, which advocates bimetallism under an international agreement, and that we were not gold monometallists." E. L. Godkin's *Post* assailed Hanna's frank explanation as "Bryanism pure and simple." Quoted in Atlanta *Constitution*, November 16, 1896.

[28] Butler to Jo A. Parker, December 19, 1896, Campaign Letterbooks, Butler MSS; Daniels' letter from Washington in Raleigh *News and Observer*, January 3, 1897.

simply carrying this variety of political primitivism to its logical end."[29]

The truth is that most Americans in 1896, regardless of which side they were on, interpreted the campaign and its issues in moral terms. Ironically, it was neither Bryan nor any of his followers who cried, "At no time since 1860 have the issues of a Presidential campaign been so distinctively moral." That was the New York *Times* in an editorial demanding that the religious journals of the churches throw their full influence "on the side of honesty and right," which meant, to the *Times*, on the side of gold.

Again, not Bryan but the *Times* asserted in a later editorial: "If there ever was a crisis in the history of this country when the teachings of the Gospel of peace and justice were involved in the duty of the citizen it is the present crisis." The metropolitan newspaper charged that the inevitable effect of Bryan's teachings was to "sow envy and uncharitableness in the hearts of large classes and to stir them to conduct which would imperil law and order." It was clearly the duty of religious teachers "in the pulpit or the press" to fight such evil influences.[30]

Eastern clergymen needed no pushes from the *Times* about their anti-Bryan zeal. Both Protestant and Catholic spokesmen took highly partisan stands with surprising boldness in 1896. "The present political discussion is moral, rather than political," a leading Baptist divine in New York city an-

[29] *The American Political Tradition and the Men Who Made It* (Vintage edition; New York, 1954), 186-205.

[30] New York *Times*, August 17, 23, 1896. It might be suggested here that some historians, who read backwards from the shabby and pathetic Bryan of the Scopes trial, do both him and millions of Americans who admired and voted for him an injustice. A great deal happened in and to the United States between 1896 and 1925, and H. L. Mencken's savagely witty portrait of Bryan, who was about to die, is not necessarily the truth about the younger presidential candidate. Bryan's simple but fervent Protestantism, for example, was not nearly as "provincial" in 1896 as it had become in 1925 and later.

nounced, "and no pulpit can keep silent when this country is threatened and the political situation casts a dark cloud over this great Republic." The same preacher soon asked from his pulpit whether "Americanism or Anarchism" should prevail. The Democratic platform threatened the stability of the republic and promised to revive Robespierre and the Jacobins. There were but two parties, this man of God concluded, "patriots and traitors."[31]

More important for the Midwest perhaps were the statements made by various prelates who were high in the hierarchy of the Roman Catholic church. Archbishop John Ireland of Minnesota declared that the Democratic platform and candidate represented a menace to the social order. Neatly introducing his own touch of the "bloody shirt," the Archbishop explained that he considered free silver, as bad as that would be, as of minor importance in comparison to the reincarnation of the doctrine of "secession" in the Democratic plank against arbitrary federal interference in local affairs. Worse than all, the Archbishop concluded, was the "spirit of socialism that permeates the whole movement that has issued from the [Democratic] convention at Chicago." It was "the 'International' of Europe, now taking body in America."

Bishop Francis F. Chatard of the diocese of Indiana then declared: "I consider that what Archbishop Ireland says about the Chicago platform . . . is exactly true." Bishop Chatard also joined in especially "deploring the arraying of class against class and the resulting bad and dangerous sentiments that may have the saddest consequences." And the Catholic bishop of Omaha, Nebraska, denied that he had called the Populists anarchists. "But I did say, and I now

---

[31] New York *Times*, July 26, August 3, 1896. For example of equally partisan sermons by other preachers in other denominations, see *ibid.*, October 5, 12, 1896.

say," he explained, "that Populists, Anarchists, and Com-
munists must not be permitted to destroy the financial credit
of our country." The Nebraska prelate, who knew Bryan and
described him as "light" and "tonguey," felt sure that the
American people would be "keen enough to escape this silver
mania" and vote for the candidates who respected American
treaties and financial honor.[32]

Republicans were naturally pleased with the clerical pro-
nouncements, especially since they had come in the campaign's midwestern battleground. Concerning Archbishop
Ireland's statement, the chief of the literary bureau in the
Republicans' Chicago headquarters noted that Ireland was
not a man "to be swayed by partisan prejudices" and whatever
he said was "bound to carry with it a great deal of weight."
Senator Jones merely commented that he had nothing to say
about the matter beyond the fact that he had no desire to
criticize the Archbishop or any other citizen "who sees fit to
express his opinions concerning National issues." The prevailing opinion in Washington political circles was reported
to be that the Archbishop's declaration would "increase the
sound-money vote in Iowa, Minnesota, Wisconsin, and Illinois 50,000 or more."[33]

George F. Washburn, the Populist leader in charge of the
party's Chicago headquarters, was himself a Catholic. Apparently, neither he nor any other Populist spokesman publicly
answered Archbishop Ireland. Although the People's party,
especially in the South, had inherited a certain rural Protestant flavor and tone from the Farmers' Alliance, Populists

[32] *Literary Digest*, XIII (October 24, 1896), 806, for Ireland; New York
Herald, October 17, 1896, for Chatard; and New York *Times*, August 9,
1896, for Bishop Newman of Omaha.

[33] New York *Times*, October 13, 1896. James H. Moynihan, *The Life of
Archbishop John Ireland* (New York, 1953), 261-63, describes Ireland's close
association with the Republican party and mentions how he helped to keep a
plank opposing any union of church and state out of the Republican platform in 1896 on the grounds that it was uncalled for and would be interpreted
as a concession to the American Protective Association.

in 1896 were concentrating on winning vital economic reforms and were not in the least interested in being drawn into
any quarrel about church-state relations. However much
Populists might have regretted the statements of Ireland and
the others, the voluminous correspondence to and from
Chairman Marion Butler's office contains no evidence of
anti-Catholicism.

Likewise the charge of anti-Semitism that various writers
have recently leveled against the Populists is one for which
absolutely no evidence can be found in the private letters that
poured into Butler's office from Populists in virtually every
state of the union. North Carolina's leading Populist newspaper, the Raleigh *Caucasian*, contained the usual stereotyped
references to the Rothschilds but the emphasis clearly was
on the fact that they were prominent world, and especially
British, bankers rather than on their Jewishness.[34]

If the Populists had been seeking scapegoats rather than
rational, governmental cures for their grievances, certainly the
irresistible target for them in the South would have been the
Negroes. But, as Professor C. Vann Woodward has pointed
out, "perhaps the most remarkable aspect of the whole
Populist movement was the resistance its leaders in the South
put up against racism and racist propaganda and the determined effort they made against incredible odds to win back
political rights for the Negroes, defend those rights against
brutal aggression, and create among their normally anti-Negro
following, even temporarily, a spirit of tolerance in which the

[34] For example, the Raleigh *Caucasian*, September 12, 1896, carried a car-
toon showing one of the Rothschilds in London sending congratulations to
McKinley. For a recent article that attacks the view that the Populists were
anti-Semitic, see Norman Pollack, "The Myth of Populist Anti-Semitism,"
American Historical Review, LXVIII (October 1962), 76-80. The most
impressive refutation of the charge of Populist anti-Semitism, however, is in
Walter T. K. Nugent, *The Tolerant Populists: Kansas Populism and Nativism*
(Chicago, 1963). Many of Professor Nugent's carefully researched conclusions concerning Kansas Populism parallel or supplement those of the writer
concerning the national party.

two races of the South could work together in one party for the achievement of common ends."³⁵

Populist efforts to win Negro votes were not, in general, successful in the South, since the Negroes, when left free to choose and to vote, usually voted Republican. The Negroes, like so many of the whites, were the victims of their history and of the traditions that clustered around Abraham Lincoln's party, the "party that freed the slaves." But through Populist-Republican cooperation in state and local elections, cooperation that was either formal and open or informal and tacit in most of the Southern states, the Populists continued to have a vital stake in the Negro's vote.

In North Carolina, with its relatively strong Republican party and its vigorous Populists, fusion for state and local purposes was formally arranged in 1896. The Democrats in North Carolina, unlike those in Georgia and Texas, proved unable to win any significant number of Negroes from their traditional loyalty to the Republicans. When the Democrats began to realize that they might lose the governorship for the first time since Reconstruction, they made a desperate last-minute effort to arouse racial passions and prejudices against the Negro minority in the state.

Furnifold M. Simmons, who was destined to lead the Tarheel Democrats in their successful "white supremacy" crusades of 1898 and 1900 and then represent the state in the United States Senate for thirty years, was unable to prevent his party's defeat in the state election of 1896. But Simmons furnished a hint of the technique that would soon lead to a second "redemption" of the state by the Democrats and to disfranchisement and legalized, mandatory segregation for

³⁵ "The Populist Heritage and the Intellectual," in *Burden of Southern History* (Baton Rouge, 1960), pp. 156-57. This brief essay of Professor Woodward's is a cogent and dispassionate refutation of the charges of anti-Semitism, isolationism, McCarthyism, etc., that were made against the Populists in the last half of the 1950's. There is also a convenient list of many of the works in which the charges were made on page 146.

the Negroes. Although himself a late and none too enthusiastic convert to Bryanism, Simmons loyally labored for the
Democratic party. In a speech delivered towards the end of
the campaign in 1896, he warned: "At one time I thought I
saw signs of a desire on the part of the colored people to vote
intelligently and to be instructed as to their best interest, and
I always took pleasure in trying to point out to them what I
thought was to their interest. . . . The day is not come and
will not come when the white people of North Carolina will
permit the colored man to rule over them. The Anglo-Saxon
neck has never yet been bended to such a yoke. . . . I am not
drawing the color line, the colored man has already drawn it,
and it is that fact, that danger, which I desire to impress
upon the white people of this country and of North Carolina."[36]

Another Democrat reported from the eastern part of the
state, where the Negro population was concentrated, that
"Hanna's black emissaries" were both numerous and effective
in persuading the Negroes that the "free silver scheme was
gotten up by the Democrats only to fool the negroes, and if
the Democrats get in power, it will be good-bye Mr. Nigger."
One of the Negro Republicans' themes was alleged to be:
"With us, my colored brethren, it is a question of free silver
or free nigger. You can take whichever you please. I am a
free nigger man myself, and therefore I am against your free
silver."[37]

The Populists' motivation in defending the Negroes' right

[36] Raleigh *News and Observer*, October 15, 1896.

[37] *Ibid.*, October 22, 1896. The intense passion and frequent violence that
characterized the election of 1896 in the South is illustrated by an incident
in which the author's great-uncle was involved: "At the opening of the polls
[for the Georgia state election] at Monte, Emanuel County, this morning,
William Durden and a negro hand walked up to vote, when a Democratic
ticket was snatched out of [the Negro's] hand by C. W. Williams, a negro
third partyite. Several Democrats rushed for him and Williams pulled his
pistol and killed S. S. Middleton. He made an effort to escape, but was over-
taken and shot to death." New York *Times*, October 8, 1896.

to vote was clearly a mixture of self-interest and more generous purposes. At any rate, the leading Tarheel Populist newspaper said a great deal in a brief space when it announced to the Democrats: "This sort of [racial] business is too old, gentlemen. Stick to the issues."[38]

The truth was that racism and nativism held little attraction in 1896 for the Populists. Desperate men in a sense, they were also politically oriented, and they hoped to capture the federal government and use it for a whole series of reforms beginning with the currency. Populists, many of whom were poorly educated and most of whom were poverty stricken, were certainly not any more immune to sin and shortcomings than anyone else. In other circumstances and times many of them, but by no means all, abandoned their hopes of reform and sought refuge in violent hates and morbid fears. But in 1896 Populists were in no mood for false issues that merely distracted from the great economic questions of the day.

In view of the denunciation of Bryan and all that he stood for by certain leaders of the Catholic church, perhaps it was not strange that in the last phase of the campaign a story began to be whispered around and finally published to the effect that the Democratic-Populist presidential candidate was in league with such anti-Catholic and nativist organizations as the American Protective Association. Actually, the A. P. A. itself had come on lean days by the time of the presidential campaign of 1896. For example, its newspaper in St. Louis, the *True American*, collapsed for want of subscribers as the campaign got underway.

But it is also clear that what was left of the organization supported McKinley and the Republicans. When John W.

[38] Raleigh *Caucasian*, October 15, 1896. On October 29 the Populist journal declared that the Democratic party in the state had remounted "its old 'riding hoss'—the howl of 'nigger' hoping that his old 'hoss' will carry them back from where they were driven. . . ."

Echols, the president of the A. P. A., was criticized by some Democrats for using the society and his office against Bryan, Nichols countered that he had only obeyed the orders of the A. P. A.'s Supreme Council in making public Bryan's attitude "toward the principles of the order." He had not done the same thing for McKinley, "because the Supreme Council had already passed upon him and his record and declared him unobjectionable to the order."[39]

Bryan's position was peculiar. He had been severely attacked by various Catholic leaders. But in Kentucky the A. P. A. was reported to have distributed widely a circular charging that Bryan had sold out to the Catholics and would be under their control if elected. Meantime, in the upper Mississippi valley the story was that Bryan, as an alleged anti-Catholic and nativist, was a member of the A. P. A. To cope with this confused and distorted situation Bryan finally moved to clear the air at the very end of the campaign: "I have not attempted to answer all of the misrepresentations which have been circulated in this campaign, but in the closing days I feel that it is necessary to call your attention to an attack which has recently been made by the enemy. . . . I am not and never have been a member of the American Protective Association or of the Junior Order of American Mechanics, or of any other society hostile to any church, religion or race; nor have I ever applied for membership in any such organization. While I am a member of the Presbyterian church, I have always believed that there should be no religious test applied in the holding of public office, and I have not allowed religious differences to affect my conduct in the discharge of the duties of public office. . . . I have tried

---

[39] St. Louis *Post-Dispatch*, August 4, 1896; New York *Times*, October 31, 1896. John Higham, *Strangers in the Land: Patterns of American Nativism, 1860-1925* (New Brunswick, N. J., 1955), 80-87, discusses the pro-Republican bias of the A. P. A., and Donald L. Kinzer, *An Episode in Anti-Catholicism: The American Protective Association* (Seattle, 1964), 224-28, describes the organization's disarray in 1896.

so far as I could to conduct this campaign in an open and
honorable way, and have insisted that those who are with us
should refrain from personal criticism of my opponent and
leave the people to pass judgment upon the principles which
we represent."[40]

BY ENTITLING his book about the campaign *The First Battle*,
Bryan meant that one defeat did not mean the loss of the war.
There would be, there had to be, another battle for silver and
all the other reforms that it symbolized. Several million
Americans, Democrats and Populists alike, shared this view.
But opinions differed sharply as to just what form the cam-
paign of 1900 should take and which party should lead the
next great effort for reform.

Marion Butler staked out the Populist claim immediately
after Bryan's defeat was clear. Deemphasizing the midroaders' disgruntlement, he insisted that the People's party
was the only one that "supported solidly and unitedly the
great and vital issues represented in the candidacy of Mr.
Bryan." The Populist chairman suggested that "had it not
been for the prejudice against the Democratic name, as well
as want of confidence in Democratic promises, for which it
must be frankly admitted past experience furnished ample
ground, a majority of the voters of the country . . . would
have cast their votes for financial reform and American independence." The defeat was not the fault of Bryan personally,
for his "remarkable and brilliant campaign" would have
aligned the majority of Americans who opposed all that
McKinley stood for "if any candidate or leader in America
could have done so under the Democratic banner." Butler's
boldly partisan conclusion was clear enough: the Populists
would be in 1900 "the nucleus around which the patriotic
hosts must and will gather to redeem a betrayed republic and

[40] New York *Times*, October 31, 1896; Bryan, *First Battle*, 593.

to restore prosperity to an oppressed and outraged people."[41]

Loyal Democrats could not be expected to accept Butler's analysis and prognosis. Governor Stone of Missouri insisted that reformers had no reason for discouragement. "A year ago the Democratic party was nearer destruction and dissolution than ever before in its history," Stone declared. "It was almost a wreck. Then the people revolted against the [Cleveland] Administration which was trying to betray the party into an abandonment of its principles." With the full power of the Cleveland administration as well as the Republicans and Gold Democrats pitted against Bryan, reformers were left "an almost impossible task in the time and with the limited means" at their disposal to organize their previously antagonistic forces. "We relied almost wholly upon the plain people, widely scattered over the country, and almost wholly unorganized at the beginning of the fight in July," the Missourian concluded. "In the face of all these advantages the goldbugs won only by the skin of their teeth."[42]

The St. Louis *Post-Dispatch* optimistically asserted that the eastern people were fundamentally "all right" and would "vote with the plain people of the West as soon as they understand the issues." If the Democratic party only had a half dozen newspapers in the East to discuss the issues and print the news fairly, the St. Louis editor argued, it could win there. Reformers in the meantime would not abandon the East but educate it "on the currency question as it was [educated] on the tariff." Another prominent Democratic newspaper, the Atlanta *Constitution*, also took the long view and emphasized that the campaign had been a profoundly educational one in which many voters "who have been brought up on war issues have had an opportunity to receive much-needed instruction."[43]

41 St. Louis *Post-Dispatch*, November 7, 1896.
42 *Ibid.*, November 8, 1896.
43 *Ibid.*, November 7, 1896; *Constitution*, November 14, 1896.

In the East and among the antisilver newspapers in general across the country, rejoicing was great that the country had escaped "anarchy" and "dishonor." But one independent newspaper in the heart of New England had the courage to pay Bryan a gracious tribute. The Springfield, Massachusetts, *Republican* declared that one could "dissent from many of his opinions and yet recognize the brilliant, persistent, desperate fortitude that has made his leadership pervasive beyond precedent." No other man, in the *Republican's* opinion, could have led the reform forces with their "disorganized and clashing interests with the same courage and untiring faith, or directed a crude campaign to any better results."[44]

The Boston correspondent of the Springfield *Republican* dared to put the matter even more bluntly when he suggested that rather than saying that "the country rose as a man" against Bryan it would be more correct to say that the Northeast rose as a mouse, for "a more frightened people as to the possible result of Bryan's election I have never seen in any of the Presidential contests that I remember." The irreverent correspondent guessed that "our Calvinistic and Federalist grandfathers were more alarmed when Jefferson was running in 1800, — and they slandered and voted against him." They had not been able to defeat the Virginian but "did their best by voting steadily for that pink of political wisdom and social morality, Aaron Burr, until wiser and calmer men further south allowed Jefferson to be chosen by the House."

Four years after that even Massachusetts had voted for Jefferson, and the newspaperman predicted that the future probably held in it a victory of the same sort for the defeated Bryan. McKinley's election had settled nothing except the breaking up of the older political parties; it certainly did not mean any permanent victory for the minority of the voters who adhered to the gold standard. Not only was Bryan's

[44] As quoted in the Atlanta *Constitution*, November 7, 1896.

record at the age of thirty-six more dazzling even than Lincoln's at the age of fifty but: "Bryan convinced the Chicago convention by his personal qualities that he was the best candidate; and as such he has dominated his party, held its discordant elements together, converted a million voters to the heresy of free silver, and got more electoral votes by 50, at least, than any other Democrat could have had in this year of party deliquescence and party treachery. He has done it too with the newspapers generally and impudently against him; with the financial interests of the country against him 10 to 1; with the whole force of the national administration wielded against him. . . . To have succeeded as he has done, under these circumstances; to have retained the respect of all his supporters, and forced the most impudent of his newspaper maligners to treat him better at the end of his contest than at the beginning—this is a personal triumph which ought to console him for the failure of too enthusiastic hopes."[45]

Bryan probably was consoled by his strong showing in the face of unprecedented difficulties, and he definitely was looking ahead to the next battle in 1900. He wrote in longhand to Butler to thank him for his services during the campaign and to request a copy of Butler's "best" photograph for inclusion in the forthcoming memoir of the campaign. In his only reference to the vice-presidential matter in the letter, Bryan declared that he believed that Butler had "made as good use as it was possible" to make of the situation.[46]

[45] As quoted in the Raleigh *News and Observer*, November 10, 1896.
[46] Bryan to Butler, December 5, 1896, Butler MSS. Bryan's book was dedicated to "three pioneers" who were "the foremost champions of bimetallism in their respective parties," Richard P. Bland, James B. Weaver, and Henry M. Teller. It also contains photographs of most of the politically prominent figures in the campaign of 1896. Concerning Watson, Bryan wrote: "I had intended to present the picture of Mr. Watson . . . together with a biographical sketch and some extracts from his campaign utterances, but have refrained from doing so at his request. I may add here that, while I did not fully agree with him as to the methods to be employed during the campaign,

Butler continued to have cordial relations with Bryan, but the Populist chairman now saw his primary obligation as being to the People's party, an obligation that should now be fulfilled in a more partisan manner than had been possible during the campaign. To preserve the party's organization and prepare it for future campaigns would require not only the most tactful handling of the midroaders but also a careful keeping of distance from Bryan and the Democrats. Butler complied with the Nebraskan's request for the photograph and other material but in doing so took advantage of the occasion to suggest that the transportation question, which Butler thought was growing more and more important, deserved treatment in Bryan's forthcoming book. Butler conceded that finance and taxation would probably always be the most vital matters, but modern conditions had made the transportation question almost equal in importance. The activities of the railroad companies in behalf of McKinley and the gold standard in the campaign just concluded had forced to the front the question of private control of a vast natural monopoly. "In fact, it seems to me," Butler argued, "that this issue will have to be fought out along with the financial question in the next national campaign."[47]

Aside from keeping his distance from Bryan and the Democrats, Butler believed that his and his party's largest problem was to stop the tendency of the southern and western wings of the party to pull further and further apart. Butler and the majority of the large North Carolina delegation to the

---

I never questioned his good faith or his right to pursue such a course as he thought to be best for the success of the reforms in which he was interested." *First Battle*, 622-23.

[47] Butler to Bryan, December 16, 1896, Campaign Letterbooks, Butler MSS. Bryan offered the Populist organization a portion of his royalties from *The First Battle* but Butler declined the offer on the grounds that Bryan belonged to the Democratic party, the Populist-Democratic alliance had been only for 1896, and the future alone would determine what course the People's party would take in 1900. Butler to G. L. Spence, April 10, 1897, *ibid.*

Populist convention at St. Louis had played an essentially national role in helping to prevent the open and final split between extreme midroaders and extreme fusionists that had been threatened. Butler still regarded the prevention of this split as his primary task.

Tom Watson, on the other hand, took his bitter grudge against Butler into the newspapers and charged that the Populist chairman was everything from "a liar and traitor" to a "selfish, unprincipled trickster." "To be foxy, double-faced, false of tongue and treacherous at heart is natural to him," the Georgian declared, "and when he betrays those who trust him and deceives those who are silly enough to take him at his word, he has no more sinned against his nature than does our friend, the 'William goat,' when it fights with its horns rather than mouth or feet." Butler, on the advice of Reed and Washburn, refrained from answering Watson's personal attack as well as from publishing a point-by-point refutation of Watson's specific charges about the recent campaign. Instead, Butler sought help wherever he could find it in checking the sectional breach that still threatened the party.[48]

In Nebraska, where most Populists accepted and even thrived under national as well as local fusion with the Democrats, J. A. Edgerton, the secretary of the Populist national executive committee, liked the idea of the nonpartisan silver clubs which Bryan had proposed as a means of keeping the educational work going and the various reform parties in harness together. Butler, fearful lest the autonomy of the People's party might be further jeopardized, was cool to the idea for the time being. To a Populist leader in Missouri who was almost ready to abandon hope of reconciling the southern midroaders, Butler wrote: "You are entirely wrong in concluding that the only Populists there are [are] in the West,

[48] Raleigh *News and Observer*, December 9, 1896; Washburn to Butler, January 13, 1897, Reed to Butler, January 15, 1897, Butler MSS.

and I must submit that it is not in the interest of party harmony for the Western Populists to become parties to making divisions between Southern and Western Populists. Instead of deserting the Southern Populists, who are Populists from principle, the Populists of the West, where the organization is strongest, should join hands with us in the fight against Hanna's agents who are masquerading as Populists."[49]

Butler was right in saying that the heart of midroad Populism was in the South, in the deep South in fact, but there were Populists in the West who, for various reasons, sympathized with and encouraged the midroaders in their angry determination to oust Butler from the party chairmanship and have the Populists nominate their own candidates for the presidency and vice presidency even if they had to do it as early as 1898, two years before the Democrats would again hold a national nomination convention. Paul Vandervoort, the Nebraskan president of the Reform Press Association, was still, as he had been during the campaign, one of the most prominent and active of the western midroaders.

Ignatius Donnelly of Minnesota hesitated and initially refused to join in the midroaders' demand for Butler's scalp, but he too eventually joined them. One of Donnelly's political allies in Minnesota was discouraged by the election results to see "the misguided fool farmers and laborers go back on their friends at the critical moment" and feared that Donnelly's grim prophesy of authoritarian rule in *Caesar's Column*, his earlier political novel, might be all too true. Donnelly obviously felt the same thing. In his melodramatic and pseudoliterary manner he confessed to his diary immediately after the election: "All our high-blown hopes have burst under us. . . . It seems useless to contest against the money-

---

[49] Edgerton to Butler, December 12, 1896, Butler to A. Rozelle of St. Louis, February 16, 1897, Campaign Letterbooks, Butler MSS. Butler called on S. F. Norton of Illinois, February 16, 1897, for help in stopping "at once this tendency of the Southern and Western Populists to pull apart."

power. Every election marks another step downward into the abyss, from which there will be no return save by fire and sword. The people are too shallow and too corrupt to conduct a republic. It will need a god come on earth, with divine power, to save them. And are they worth saving? Will they stay saved? . . . Never were the circumstances more favorable for success. We had a splendid candidate and he had made a gigantic campaign; the elements of reform were fairly united; and the depression of business universal, and yet in spite of it all the bankrupt millions voted to keep the yoke on their own necks. . . . I tremble for the future."[50]

Donnelly's dire forebodings for the future were only slightly more pointless than all of Butler's efforts to preserve a national Populist party and all of the midroaders' efforts to force drastic and premature decisions on whatever fragment of the party that might follow them. Although men at that time could hardly be expected to have realized the fact immediately, the climax of Populism, the zenith of its impact on the nation's history, had been reached in the campaign of 1896. Events totally unforeseen at the time and certainly beyond the control of the Populists brought the gradual death of the party.

In the first place, prosperity did return to the nation in the last years of the decade, and Populism, which had reached its greatest national strength after the panic of 1893, could retain neither its militancy nor its membership without the sharp prodding of massive poverty. The brighter economic scene after 1897 did not mean that the fundamental ills which afflicted farmers and laborers had been cured in any perma-

---

[50] F. C. Culver to Donnelly, November 10, 1896, Donnelly's diary entry for November 6, 1896, Donnelly MSS. One of Henry D. Lloyd's radical friends was less philosophical when he wrote: "A really popular measure of reform would be one that would make the poor rich and the rich immensely wealthy. Any levelling up and down measure will meet condemnation from the top and bottom and be given the cold hands by the middle class." A. B. Adair to Lloyd, November 11, 1896, Lloyd MSS.

nent way, for they had not. Both groups still suffered from the grievances that had inspired the Populists' many-sided platform concerning currency and banking, transportation, the influx of cheap immigrant labor, and other matters. But the economy had ground its way through the painful cycle of deflation, mass unemployment, and bankruptcy and had finally come upon better times. The blunting of the sharp edge of the depression spelled death for the People's party as a major force in American political life.

On the specific issue of free silver, the denouement is well known. The increase in the volume of the currency and relief from the acute deflation which reformers had sought through silver came about in the years immediately after the election —but came through the decisive increase in the world's supply of gold. By 1897 the output of gold was double the total amount produced in 1890, and by 1899 it was on the way to trebling the figure for 1890. By 1900, when the Republicans enacted the Gold Standard Act, even the most ardent silverite of 1896 had to admit that the old issue had lost its political potency.[51]

The Spanish-American War was another development that hastened the disappearance of Populism. The humanitarian fever to help liberate the ill-treated Cubans hit Populists no less than most other Americans in 1897-1898. "The blare of the bugle drowned the voice of the Reformer," as Tom Watson put it, and with "the cannon-boom shaking the world, men had no ear for political economy—or economy of any other sort."[52] Before the "splendid little war" with Spain could be decently concluded, the United States had embarked on the adventuresome course of making colonies out of the Philippines, Guam, Puerto Rico, and Hawaii, and the nation was plunged into a great debate about imperialism.

[51] Hicks, *Populist Revolt*, 389.
[52] *Watson's Jeffersonian Magazine*, V (October 1910), 817.

The return of prosperity, the increase in the gold supply and the decline in appeal of the reform groups' common denominator of free silver, the popular crusade to liberate Cuba, and the ensuing imperialism—all of these things combined to kill Populism on the national scene. On the state level there were other developments that helped destroy the third party. In the West local fusion was the bridge by which many Populists gradually moved into the Democratic party, but in the South such a step was one that many Populists could never bring themselves to take. The fate of the Populists in the southern states is perhaps best illustrated by what happened to the vigorous party in North Carolina.

There in 1898, when Cleveland Democrats and Bryan Democrats could cooperate in the absence of a presidential election, Furnifold M. Simmons, aided by Josephus Daniels and others, led the "white man's party" in a "white supremacy crusade" to regain control of the legislature. Populist-Republican or "Fusion" rule in the state had brought with it a highly limited amount of office holding by Negroes, mostly in the eastern counties and in minor local offices. But the mere fact of large-scale Negro voting combined with the office holding allowed the Democrats to revive the Reconstruction cry of "nigger domination." Making a calculated play on racial passion and prejudice and using mounted and armed "Red Shirts" in various counties, the Democrats succeeded in recapturing the legislature.

In 1900 the Democrats not only recaptured the governorship but, through an even more violent and revolutionary process than in 1898, secured the enactment of a state constitutional amendment that effectively disfranchised most Negro voters. Butler and many other Populists joined with Republicans in the state to fight these Democratic measures. Butler even secured help from some of the Texas Populists, such as Harry Tracy and "Stump" Ashby, in the crucial state election of 1900. But Tarheel Democrats were ruthless in their determination to "redeem" the state once and for all and to end all threats to the hegemony of the "white man's party."

Butler received hundreds of letters in the closing years of the century that poignantly suggest how the fate of the southern Populists and that of the Negroes had become intertwined. Requesting strict privacy, one rural Negro wrote: "A large number white men Democrats come to my little store & drove me inside & said not come any more, but my wife heard what they were doing & she & her aunt come down to the store & demanded that they [stop] it & I be let to go home with her, & so they let me go home & and all night they were shoting around my store, & run a rope from my store across the street & made a coffin & put on the rope & marked on [it] dead negro, this morning I cut the rope into, & they cursed & abused me, & I went in store & they demanded that I not come out any moore, & said that I had to leave here, did't I would see what become of me, that one O'clock today that they were going to bury me in that coffin & preach my furnerl, & so on, that I could *leave* & live, or *stay* & be *burried*. So what must I do? & what can I do? Is there a place you could put me in or give me something to do? I am in a terrible condision now, & must do something."[53]

Another foe of the disfranchising amendment reported that about fifty Redshirt Democrats visited Negro homes in the community, warned the Negroes not to dare to try to register, and shot a hundred or more pistol shots in the air. The Democrats were said to "swair vengins against any Justice of the peace that offers to assist or help the negro to register or . . . to fill out the blanks that the Populist and Republicans has been sending out." The frightened registrar was said to

53 S. S. Strother of Eureka, Wayne County, North Carolina, to Butler, August 3, 1900, Butler MSS.

keep a pistol lying on the table beside him but "if there is any federal law to resort to he ought to be attended to at once."[54]

The white Populists in North Carolina who followed Butler in vigorously fighting the Democrats and their disfranchisement of the Negroes did not do so out of liberal convictions on the race question. Political circumstances and expediency led the white Populists to side with the Negro. Thus, one Populist wrote: "I am not in favour of the negro but I do beleave in giving the pore negro his dues. I live in Dunn N. C. where they say you [Butler] wold never be aloud to speak in no more. And this negro that I want to tel you [about] went to register and [they] wold not let him and he come to me and told me about it." Another white Populist reported that the local "white supremacy" clubs admitted boys from age twelve on up and trained them "to have prejudice towards his fellow man who differs in opinion with him." "I have thought this was a God fearing people," he concluded, "but it seems as if the devil has gotten possession of their minds and hearts."[55]

The frauds and violence that accompanied the return to complete political power of the Tarheel Democrats and their victory for disfranchisement in 1900 threw the remaining Populists into despair. One declared after the state election that he felt he had "nothing to vote tor and don't know that I ever shall vote again." Another requested Butler to send a copy of the national Republican platform. The irony of the total political situation in 1900 was not lost on the Populists:

[54] A. D. Sprivey of Ellerbe, North Carolina, to Butler, July 20, 1900, *ibid.* N. C. Cooper of Nashville, North Carolina, wrote Butler on August 4, 1900, immediately after the state election, that the Democrats refused to let Republicans register and walked around on election day with pistols showing. "I hope my dear Senator when Congress meets that you will pass a law that soldiers shall count the votes of every county in the state. . . . It was a shame and disgrace to see how Christian people did in this election." *Ibid.*

[55] Neal A. Butler of Dunn, North Carolina, to Butler, July 16, 1900, W. H. Brown of Rosemead, North Carolina, to Butler, July 5, 1900, Butler MSS.

while Bryan and the national Democratic party staunchly opposed the denial of liberty to the Filipinos, Bryan's party in North Carolina and other southern states resorted to violent, even revolutionary, tactics to disfranchise the Negro.[56]

Despite the irony, Butler did not immediately join the Republican party, as many other Populists did in North Carolina after the state election of 1900. Unwilling to ignore the national issues that were before the country, Butler continued to serve as a leader in the national Populist party and campaigned in South Dakota and other western states for the Populist presidential nominee in 1900, who was once again William Jennings Bryan.[57]

Butler had helped earlier in the year to have the Populist national convention nominate Bryan, even before the Democrats could do so, and to name as his running mate Charles A. Towne, a Silver Republican of Minnesota. When the Democrats nominated Adlai E. Stevenson of Illinois as Bryan's running mate and Towne withdrew, Butler and other Populist fusionists stuck to Bryan in preference to McKinley or the midroad Populist ticket that consisted of Wharton Barker of Pennsylvania and Ignatius Donnelly of Minnesota for the presidency and vice presidency respectively.[58]

[56] J. E. Avery to Butler, August 5, 1900, Joseph W. Farabow to Butler, August 4, 1900, *ibid.* The Raleigh *Caucasian* on August 16, 1900, declared that Josephus Daniels' *News and Observer* was so mesmerized by the race issue that "if it should stumble upon a single truth, it would fall over it and then get up and swear she had been assaulted by a 'nigger.' "

[57] The Aberdeen, S. D., *Sentinel,* as quoted in the Raleigh *Caucasian,* October 25, 1900, reported that Butler emphasized in his speeches the necessity of controlling the trusts and anti-imperialism. The same issue of Butler's paper carried a story entitled "Cotton Is King" about the high price commanded by the southern staple. After the feverish state election, the *Caucasian* often referred to the widespread apathy toward the national election.

[58] The best account of the quarrels between the Populist factions after 1896 is still Hicks, *Populist Revolt,* 380-403. Ridge, *Donnelly,* 366 ff., traces the Minnesotan's role, and Woodward, *Watson,* 355-63, treats the 1904 campaign when the midroaders finally had what little was left of the party to themselves and nominated Tom Watson for the presidency.

That some Populists "soured" in the twentieth century and became hatemongers or reactionary demagogues is a familiar fact. Tom Watson, with his later career as baiter of Negroes and Jews and Catholics, is the most famous example of the degeneration of Populism. But the case of Watson and a few others like him should not lead to the conclusion that this was the typical pattern. Although statistical and biographical information is not available to prove the point, there were probably just as many or more Populists like Butler who remained interested in reforms, especially for the farmers of the nation, and who never resorted to hate campaigns against religious or racial minorities as an outlet for frustration and despair.

By 1904 Butler had become a Republican, both in North Carolina and the nation. Theodore Roosevelt was president and was nominated to succeed himself, while the Democrats in running Alton B. Parker of New York had in one sense reverted to their habits of the Cleveland era. Butler and the several thousand other Tarheel Populists who became Republicans enthusiastically supported Roosevelt, even in the famous split in the party in 1912. And after Woodrow Wilson's victory, as the Progressive Movement approached its climax in the New Freedom, Butler's wife remembered the 1890's when an earlier reform effort had failed and wryly noted: "Twenty years ago, when we were advocating the things that the whole country is standing for now, we were called 'long-haired cranks.' Does it not seem funny how soon people forget, or, rather, I might say, how long it takes them to learn?"[59]

Though too many complacent observers at the time, as well as some historians, did see the Populists as mere "long-haired cranks," from the climax of Populism in 1896 to the begin-

[59] Mrs. Butler to F. H. Hoover, November 9, 1912, in the Mrs. Marion (Florence Faison) Butler MSS, Southern Historical Collection, University of North Carolina Library.

nings of Progressivism in the early Twentieth century was not so long a period. The Populists, caught in the changed economic and international circumstances of the last years of the old century, had finally been forced to "close their academy." But they had provided political education for many Americans, leaders as well as the led, education about the need for expanded governmental action, state and federal, to redress the economic grievances that afflicted both the old majority who were farmers and the rising class of the nation's future who were urban industrial workers.

Note on Sources

IN VIEW of the footnotes scattered throughout the text and the analytical index that also covers the notes, a listing of all the printed sources that are cited hardly seems necessary; but a brief description of the chief manuscript and newspaper sources that were used, together with a critical discussion of the key printed studies that bear on the role of the Populists in the election of 1896, might be helpful to other historians.

MANUSCRIPTS

Marion Butler Papers—This large holding in the Southern Historical Collection of the University of North Carolina Library furnished the documentary backbone for the two chapters dealing with the Populist part in the campaign of 1896 and had valuable material for the other three chapters as well. Chronologically arranged in folders, hundreds of letters from Populists, important ones as well as unknown ones, give incomparable information on state and national aspects of the political battle. Two large letterbooks, together with scattered carbon copies, give the views of Butler and of the national executive committee of the Populist party. Butler's incoming correspondence dealt extensively with North Carolina politics, so the historian who wishes to concentrate on the national aspects of the campaign must go through many folders in which national and purely local letters are mixed.

Thomas E. Watson Papers—Also in the Southern Historical

Collection of the University of North Carolina Library, this is not a rich source for 1896. There are several letters from Butler and other members of the national committee to Watson and the one tantalizing letter from Evan P. Howell to Watson about the mysterious, abortive negotiations aimed at conciliating Tom Watson.

Ignatius Donnelly Papers—This collection in the State Historical Society of Minnesota has been extensively used by historians for many years, but Donnelly's diary furnished a unique and still fresh view of Bryan and the campaign. The incoming letters also afford one of the best insights into the thinking of many northern Populists. Donnelly's scrapbooks afford a handy sampling of midwestern newspapers.

Henry Demarest Lloyd Papers—Caro Lloyd's published biography contains excerpts from many of Lloyd's influential letters, and historians have long found them useful. But the extensive collection in the State Historical Society of Wisconsin is still well worth studying, and letters to Lloyd, especially from his sister and from Florence Kelley, proved to be illuminating.

William Jennings Bryan Papers—Although this collection in the Library of Congress is notoriously skimpy for 1896, there were several items, including letters from Arthur Sewall of Maine and Governor Stone of Missouri, that proved useful.

NEWSPAPERS

The absence of any official record of the Populist convention in St. Louis forces the historian to rely exclusively on newspaper sources and to do so with considerable care in view of the hostility of many reporters and editors to the Populists.

The St. Louis *Globe-Democrat, Republic,* and *Post-Dispatch* contained the most detailed, continuous accounts of the convention. The last-named newspaper also proved helpful in its coverage of the national campaign as well as of the local variations in several western states. Friendly to Bryan and silver, the *Post-Dispatch* gradually grew more appreciative of the Populist role during the campaign.

Marion Butler's Raleigh *Caucasian* was only a weekly, but eye-witness reports of the St. Louis convention by the editor, Hal Ayer, were revealing, and many pertinent stories and editorials from large dailies across the nation were reprinted during the campaign, to the great convenience of the historian. There are files of the *Caucasian* in the Duke University Library, but the most complete file seems to be that in the State Library in Raleigh, North Carolina; the Department of Archives and History has recently microfilmed the paper.

Josephus Daniels also wrote first-hand accounts of the Populist convention for his Raleigh *News and Observer,* and the Populist role in the campaign received extensive coverage, favorable as far as the national campaign was concerned and hostile with reference to the Populist-Republican cooperation within North Carolina. The Atlanta *Constitution,* another Democratic daily, was lively, good on national coverage, and especially helpful for Watson and the Georgia Populists.

Of the New York newspapers, the *Times* and the *Herald* were used the most extensively, the former furnishing a conservative, eastern perspective as well as good national coverage. Since several of the newspapers that were read reprinted extensively from the New York *World* and the *Journal* those two sources were used only indirectly, as were many other newspapers that are mentioned in the text and notes.

SELECTED PRINTED STUDIES

No attempt is made here to offer an exhaustive bibliography on either Populism or the election of 1896. Rather, the purpose is to discuss briefly selected articles and books, especially the newer ones, that bear directly on the role of the Populists in the Battle of the Standards. The starting point for any study of Populism is still John D. Hicks, *The Populist Revolt* (St. Paul, 1931; Lincoln, Nebr., 1961), which includes a valuable bibliography and is, despite a debatable interpretation of the Populists in 1896, an excellent, pioneering book.

Surely for some time henceforth the starting point for an understanding of the election of 1896 will be Stanley L. Jones, *The Presidential Election of 1896* (Madison, 1964). This comprehensive and careful study appeared after the manuscript for this monograph had been not only completed but revised. While the Populists are not of course spotlighted in *The Presidential Election of 1896*, they are, together with all the parties and leaders, discussed dispassionately. Perhaps the most important difference in interpretation between Professor Jones' book and this one is that he sees the People's party as more or less doomed as a separate organization after the reformers had captured the Democratic party and nominated Bryan. The documentation in *The Presidential Election of 1896* is meticulous, but the brief bibliography does not include any of the secondary literature. For that, Paul W. Glad, *McKinley, Bryan, and the People* (Philadelphia, 1964), is useful; although his version of the Populist role in 1896 borrows heavily from Henry Demarest Lloyd's socialist view, Professor Glad's brief synthesis is readable and well adapted to classroom use. Another attempt at an even briefer synthesis is Harold U. Faulkner, *Politics, Reform, and Expansion, 1890-1900* (New York, 1959), which also has a useful bibliography.

Next to Professor Hicks, the most influential student of Populism has been C. Vann Woodward, and his first book, *Tom Watson: Agrarian Rebel* (New York, 1938, 1955), rightfully enjoys a reputation as an artistic model of its kind. With all its merits, however, the biography presents the tangled events of 1896 essentially from Watson's highly personal and strange point of view. Professor Woodward's *Origins of the New South, 1877-1913* (Baton Rouge, 1951), has less of a pro-Watson bias concerning the Populists and includes an indispensable bibliography where the numerous state studies of Populism, among other things, may be conveniently found. His essay on "The Populist Heritage and the Intellectual" in *The Burden of Southern History* (Baton Rouge, 1960), concedes that American reform movements "have all had their seamy side and their share of the irrational, the zany, and the retrograde," yet Professor Woodward refutes the charges of anti-Semitism, proto-McCarthyism, nativism, and many other unlovely things that became fashionable to say about the Populists in the 1950's. There is a convenient list of a number of the more important works in which the charges were made on page 146.

A new study of the leading anti-Catholic organization of the era, Donald L. Kinzer, *An Episode in Anti-Catholicism: The American Protective Association* (Seattle, 1964), also suggests that the A. P. A. made little or no headway in Populist ranks, even where it was strongest in the Midwest, and that among the various regions the nativist group found least success in the South. The most recent biography of an important Populist leader who has figured largely in the criticisms of Populism is Martin Ridge, *Ignatius Donnelly: The Portrait of a Politician* (Chicago, 1962).

Peter Viereck, Talcott Parsons, Seymour M. Lipset, and a number of other writers echoed the attacks on the Populists, but the most influential historian among the critics of the 1950's was Professor Richard Hofstadter. In his *Age of Reform, From Bryan to F. D. R.* (New York, 1955), he elaborately qualified his strictures against the agrarians, yet the prevailing impression left was that they really were, despite all the reservations, anti-Semites, zenophobes, and perhaps even proto-fascists who sought not specific political reforms for concrete economic grievances but rather scapegoats as psychological outlets for their essentially irrational drives.

Despite the brilliance of his writing, the fact remains that Professor Hofstadter built elaborate theses about the Populists that were based largely on a few allusions in third-rate political novels by Ignatius Donnelly of Minnesota and a small group of other, more obscure agrarian writers of the 1890's. At the opposite pole in research technique and probably the most effective rehabilitation of the Populists that has appeared to date is Walter T. K. Nugent, *The Tolerant Populists: Kansas Populism and Nativism* (Chicago, 1963). Professor Nugent has combed the files of scores of newspapers, manuscript collections, election returns, census data, and other such sources to get impressively close to the grassroots of Populism in Kansas, the western center of the movement. His principal conclusions are: 1) that the Kansas Populists, far from being nativistic, were "friendlier and more receptive to foreign persons and foreign institutions than the average of their contemporary political opponents"; 2) that rather than being neurotically "conspiracy-minded" they were concerned with tangible facts, especially economic ones; 3) that they "got along well with their Jewish neighbors and consistently refrained from extending their dislike of certain financiers, who happened to be Jews [the Rothschilds], to Jews in general"; 4) that the Populists as a group supported intervention in Cuba on humanitarian rather than jingoistic grounds and "strongly opposed the imperialism that the war engendered"; and 5) that Populist fusion with the Bryan Democracy in 1896 was not a betrayal of reform principles but a "legitimate means to the accomplishment of real, if limited, reform."

Professor Norman Pollack develops a similar thesis in *The Populist Response to Industrial America: Midwestern Populist Thought* (Cambridge, Mass., 1962), although he uses a different approach from Professor Nugent and has chosen to write intellectual history with a minimum of attention to specific political developments. Professor Pollack concludes that Populism, far from being retrogressive and anti-Semitic, was a progressive, even a radical social force that accepted industrialization and sought a political alliance with urban labor. Emphasizing the fact that Populists did not sullenly resist social change and hanker nostalgically for a bygone era, he tentatively suggests that the failure of the farmers and urban laborers to coalesce in 1896 may have been more the fault of the latter than of the former and that Populist fusion with the Democrats in 1896 was "the last chance to advance radicalism" rather than a grab for spoils or a humiliating capitulation for the Populists.

The usefulness of Professor Pollack's study is limited by the fact that he chose to ignore the southern Populists, whom Professor Woodward has portrayed as more radical than their western allies. There is also a certain confusion in *The Populist Response to Industrial America* as to the role of Henry D. Lloyd. At one point Professor Pollack writes a bit defensively that Lloyd "after all, *was* a Populist." But later there is the emphatic assertion that, "Populism was certainly not Marxism; its vision of America was not socialized production and the collective farm."

Henry Demarest Lloyd has been and will probably continue to be a fascinating, central figure in the history of Populism. In the first place, aside from his active participation as a leader of the party in Chicago and Illinois, Lloyd's impressive intellectual and literary powers have made him a major source used by most of the students of Populism on the national level. His article on "The Populists at St. Louis," *Review of Reviews*, XIV (September 1896), is one of the handiest and most widely cited of all the contemporary accounts. Passages from many of his highly quotable letters, including the famous one where he portrayed free silver as the "cow-bird of the reform movement," have long been available in Caro A. Lloyd, *Henry Demarest Lloyd, 1847-1903* (2 vols.; New York, 1912). The most perceptive study of the Populist phase of Lloyd's career is in Chester M. Destler, *American Radicalism, 1865-1901* (New London, Conn., 1946). This earlier work seems sounder, at least where Populism is concerned, than Professor Destler's more recent biography, *Henry Demarest Lloyd and the Empire of Reform* (Philadelphia, 1963). In the biography Professor Destler is not convincing in his chapter on the Populist crisis of 1896 when he concludes, without offering any evidence for the charge, that "the great business interests whom Lloyd's crusade for social justice had challenged since 1888, via the agency of the free-silver Bryan Populists," blocked Lloyd's plan to carry the Populist convention at St. Louis for "Labor-Populism and antimonopoly from the floor."

Although Lloyd had no use for William Jennings Bryan and Lloyd's predilections on that score have been shared by a large number of later historians, the Nebraskan is inevitably a pivotal figure in any discussion of the Populist party's actions in 1896. The lack of a reliable biography of Bryan has long been a major gap in our historiography. Paolo E. Coletta has already published a number of useful articles, including "Bryan, Cleveland, and the Disrupted Democracy, 1890-1896," *Nebraska History*, XLI (March 1960), and he reportedly will publish, possibly even before this appears in print, the first volume in a projected two-volume biography. Paul W. Glad, *The Trumpet Soundeth: William Jennings Bryan and His Democracy, 1896-1912* (Lincoln, Nebr., 1960) is an interpretative, readable essay; but perhaps the most widely read and influential portrait of Bryan in recent years is the chapter entitled "William Jennings Bryan: The Democrat as Revivalist" in Richard Hofstadter, *The American Political Tradition and the Men Who Made It* (Vintage edition; New York, 1954). There the Great Commoner is variously described in a witty and unfair manner as "a circuit-riding evangelist in politics," "a boy who never left home," and "a provincial politician following a provincial populace in provincial prejudices." Although Professor Jones in the above-mentioned *Presidential Election of 1896* also sees Bryan as "one of the last among nineteenth-century men to give shape and voice to the agrarian political ideologies of Jefferson and Jackson," he at least does not start with the shabby, old Bryan of the Scopes trial and read backwards nor does he employ a subtle double standard to hit at Bryan's admittedly simple Protestantism. Bryan's Presbyterianism probably had no more to do with his reform ideas than the Catholicism or Jewishness of various political leaders of a later generation had to do with their public stands.

The book which Bryan, with the help of his wife, put together immediately after his defeat for the presidency, *The First Battle: A Story of the Campaign of 1896* (Chicago, 1897), is useful not only for the straightforward narrative but also for the many documents, such as party platforms and speeches, that are included. James A. Barnes, "Myths of the Bryan Campaign," *Mississippi Valley Historical Review*, XXXIV (December 1947), is an important revisionist analysis that attempted to correct many of the persistent misconceptions about the Nebraskan and the silver issue. The role of another preeminent Democratic reformer, Governor Altgeld of Illinois, is described in Harvey Wish, "John Peter Altgeld and the Background of the Campaign of 1896," *Mississippi Valley Historical Review*, XXIV (March 1938).

For those conservative Democrats in 1896 who much preferred McKinley and the high tariff to Bryan and silver, Allan Nevins, *Grover Cleveland, A Study in Courage* (New York, 1933), is standard but biased in favor of its subject and his policies. Horace S. Merrill, *Bourbon Leader: Grover Cleve-*

land and the Democratic Party (Boston, 1957), is much more
critical of Cleveland's party-splitting "courage," and J.
Rogers Hollingsworth, *The Whirligig of Politics: The Democracy of
Cleveland and Bryan* (Chicago, 1963), treats the two glaringly
dissimilar Democrats with cool impartiality in his analysis of
the party's vicissitudes between 1893 and 1904.

The minority of Republicans who were reform-minded in
1896 is best approached through Elmer Ellis, *Henry Moore
Teller: Defender of the West* (Caldwell, Idaho, 1941) and
particularly the same author's article, "The Silver Republicans
in the Election of 1896," *Mississippi Valley Historical Review*,
XVIII (March 1932). Gilbert C. Fite, "Republican Strategy
and the Farm Vote in the Presidential Campaign of 1896,"
American Historical Review, LXV (July 1960), focuses on
the agrarians in the crucial north central states and the
Republican approach to them.

Herbert Croly, *Marcus Alonzo Hanna* (New York, 1919),
is still the most helpful study of the sagacious Republican
campaign manager, but two newer biographies of McKinley
have appeared: Margaret Leach, *In the Days of McKinley*
(New York, 1959), presents a colorful narrative emphasizing
the personal aspect while H. Wayne Morgan, *William Mc-
Kinley and His America* (Syracuse, 1963), is more useful to
the scholar. Professor Morgan has also edited a volume of
essays, *The Gilded Age: A Reappraisal* (Syracuse, 1963),
treating various aspects of the period; one of the most helpful
of these essays is Paolo E. Coletta, "Greenbackers, Goldbugs,
and Silverites: Currency, Reform and Policy, 1860-1897."

Although economists appear more sharply and certainly less
intelligibly divided than historians about the economic aspects
of the late nineteenth century, Milton Freedman and Anna
Jacobson Schwartz in *A Monetary History of the United
States, 1867-1960* (Princeton, 1963), present the most recent
scholarly, and controversial, analysis that indirectly supports

those reformers of the 1890's who emphasized the volume of the currency as a prime factor in the economic health of the nation.

Finally, a trail-blazing article that appeared more than two decades ago still proves fundamentally important, William Diamond, "Urban and Rural Voting in 1896," *American Historical Review*, XLVI (January 1941). Carl N. Degler, "American Political Parties and the Rise of the City: An Interpretation," *Journal of American History*, LI (June 1964), offers a provocative view of the trend toward Republican primacy that began with the elections of 1894 and 1896 and is but one of the more recent studies which builds in part on the foundation laid by Professor Diamond.

Index

ABOUT THE AUTHOR

ROBERT F. DURDEN, an associate professor in the Department of History at Duke University, was educated at Emory University and at Princeton, where he received his Ph.D. degree. He is the author of a number of articles in scholarly journals as well as studies on James Shepherd Pike and on a once-famous interstate lawsuit concerning Reconstruction bonds and North Carolina politics.